Popular Teaching Resources

Art Lessons

Grades 3-4

Monica Whatley

Printed in China

Contents

Guidelines for Use

This resource book contains three sections:

- Core Units
- Checklists
- Project Ideas

Each **Core Unit** is made up of an information sheet, two follow-up worksheets, and an activity for the entire class to do together. You will see that in all of the units, "Name", "Date", and the unit topic appear in each follow-up worksheet so that each one can stand on its own. There is more than one way to present each unit in the book. Here are two that may work for you: (1) give your students the lesson and the worksheets at the same time and let them work on both simultaneously, followed by the class activity; (2) give just the lesson and class activity one day and ask your students to underline key words and ideas or take notes as you talk about the subject, and then give them a worksheet the next day as a quiz.

The **Checklists** allow both you and your students to mark the students' progress and recognize which areas may need more study or attention.

The **Project Ideas** give students the opportunity to work creatively on projects that will help them develop their understanding of the material in many of the Core Units.

Happy teaching!

Music

Name: Date:

Music Basics

Objective: *To demonstrate the difference between the terms "beat" and "rhythm", and to indicate the dynamics heard in familiar music with appropriate arm movements*

Think of the clear, even beats of your heart. In music, the **beat** is like your heart's **steady pulse**. When you clap your hands along to a song, you clap the beat.

The **rhythm** is the **pattern of long and short sounds** that drives the music forward. *A rum, pitter patter pang, a rum pitter patter pang* is a rhythm.

If you run up a hill, your heart beats faster. In music, this would be a change in **tempo**, or the speed of a piece. When you are frightened, your heart seems to beat loudly. **Dynamics** are the different degrees of volume of a piece.

Listen to *Peter and the Wolf* by Sergei Prokofiev. Make big movements, like the conductor of a symphony, when the music gets louder. As the music quiets, make your arm movements smaller and smaller. Be the "conductor" for *O Canada* and other very familiar pieces.

Name: Date:

Music Basics

A. Do each activity with the given beat.

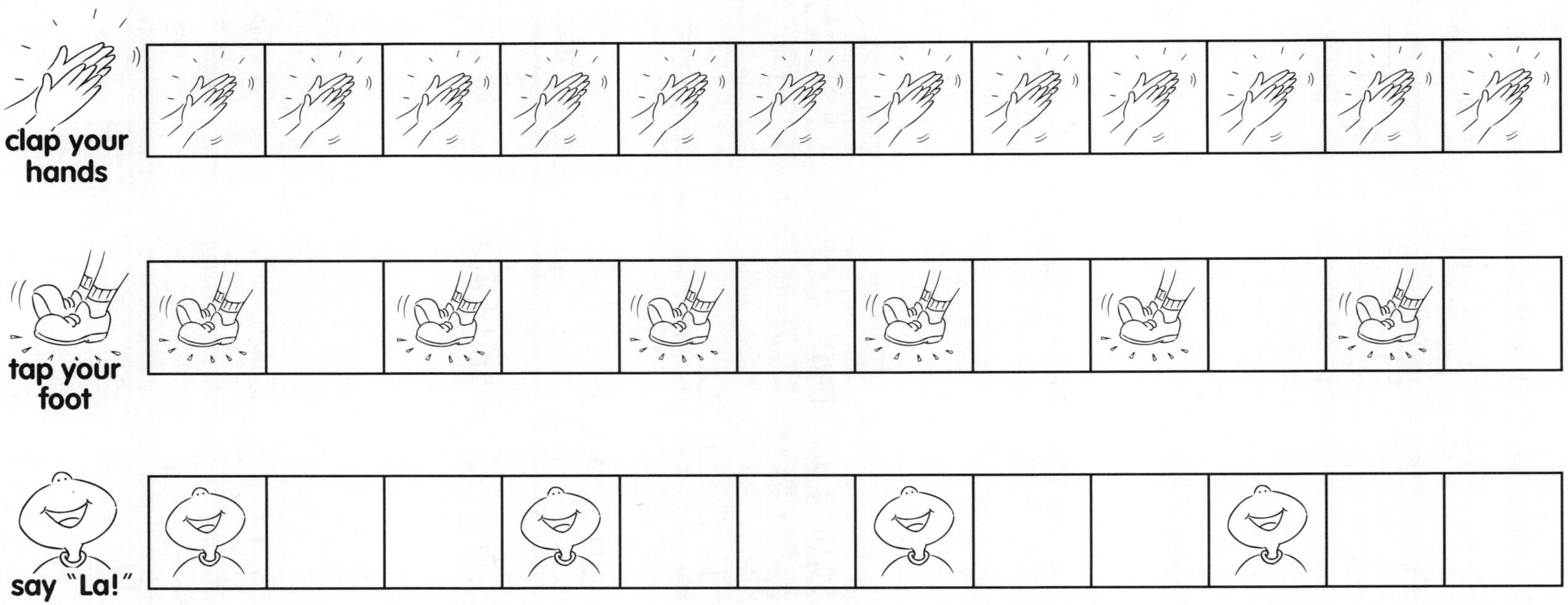

1. clap your hands
2. tap your foot
3. say "La!"

B. Listen to your teacher's clapping. Put a checkmark in the boxes to show when your teacher claps.

1.

2.

Name: Date:

Music Basics

Follow the movements when singing *O Canada*. Cut and paste the movements in the boxes. Then pretend to be a conductor, and lead your class to sing it again.

My Piece

O Canada!

Our home and native land!

True patriot love in all thy sons command.

With glowing hearts we see thee rise,

The True North strong and free!

From far and wide, O Canada,

We stand on guard for thee.

God keep our land glorious and free!

O Canada,

We stand on guard for thee.

O Canada,

We stand on guard for thee.

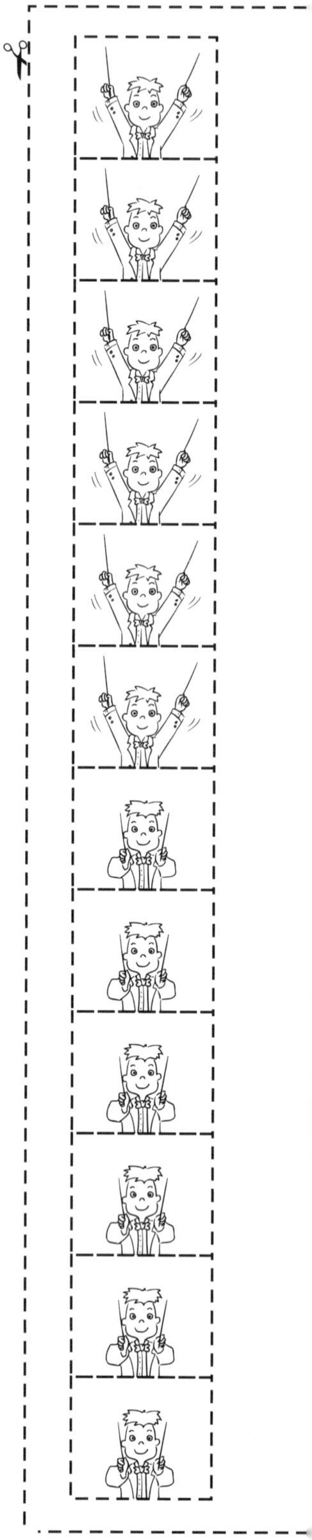

Name: Date:

Music Basics

Drum Beat

Materials:

- empty margarine containers (lid off) or plastic flower pots
- chopsticks or wooden spoons
- familiar music of teacher's choice

Motivation:

To identify the beat, rhythm, dynamics, and tempo in familiar pieces of music using a make-shift drum, and to perform simple rhythmic patterns while paying particular attention to suitable dynamics and tempo

What to Do:

1. Flip the containers or flower pots over onto a flat surface to act as drums.
2. Practise beating the drums with chopsticks or wooden spoons. Try to make a steady beat by calling out slowly 1, 2, 1, 2, 1, 2, 1, 2...
3. Play the music and have the students hit their drums to the constant, even beat. Try this with a variety of pieces.
4. Have one side of the class sing a familiar tune, while the other side beat their drums.
5. Switch and increase the tempo (speed) of the singers. Continue switching, adjusting the tempo and dynamics (making it faster/slower and louder/softer).
6. Group the students in twos, and have them use their hands to clap out the rhythm of a familiar song. See if their partners can guess the title (e.g. *Happy Birthday*, *Hickory Dickory Dock*, or *Old MacDonald*).

Discussion:

- Was it easier to keep the beat when the tempo was slower?
- Did the volume of the song affect the beat?
- How were the clapping of the rhythm and the drum beat different?

Name: Date:

The Notes and Rests

Objective: *To recognize that sounds and silences of different durations are represented in writing by symbols: whole notes, half-notes, quarter notes, and eighth-notes*

How can musicians all over the world learn the same song without having heard it? Music has both sounds and silences that can be recorded on paper as notes and rests. When musicians look at these symbols, they know what and for how long to play, sing, or rest!

Long and short sounds in music are represented by **notes**. We divide these notes into groups, or **measures**, so that the music is easier to read. If there are four beats in a measure, and the quarter note gets the beat, it is called **4/4 time**.

A whole note looks just as it sounds – like a hole. It is like a donut, with nothing in the middle. It gets **four beats** or counts in 4/4 time. A whole rest looks like a little, filled-in rectangle.

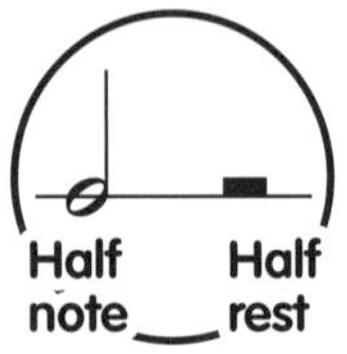

A half note or rest receives **two beats** or counts. Two of these can fill a measure in 4/4 time.

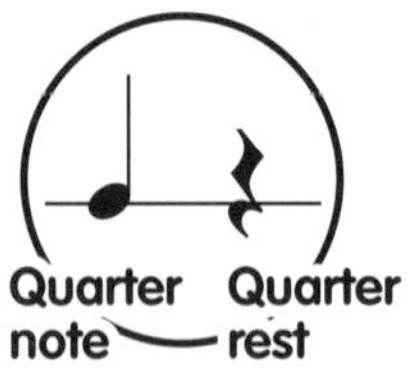

A quarter note or rest gets **one beat** in 4/4 time. Four quarter notes fit in one measure.

Half a beat can be represented by an eighth note or rest. Up to eight eighth notes fit in a measure in 4/4 time.

> *Thanks to these symbols, we can enjoy the music of artists who lived hundreds of years ago, like Beethoven, Handel, and Bach. We can also write our own music to share with others!*

Name: Date:

The Notes and Rests

A. Copy each note and rest three times.

1. whole note
2. whole rest
3. half note
4. half rest
5. quarter note
6. quarter rest
7. eighth note
8. eighth rest

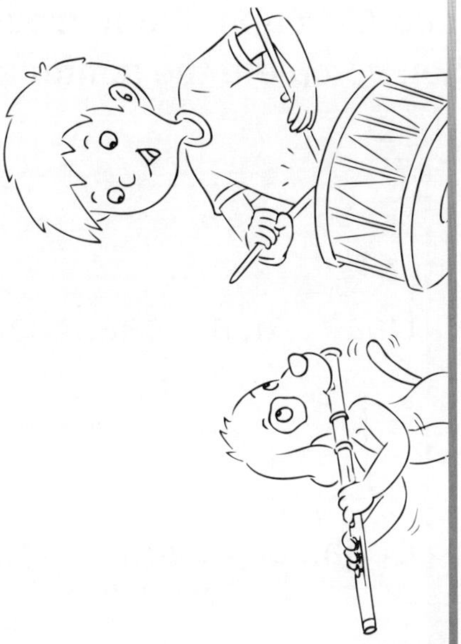

B. Identify the rests and notes.

Name: Date:

The Notes and Rests

Divide your class into 4 groups. Each group is assigned to a note and takes turns singing "Daaa". Then complete the sentences with the correct notes.

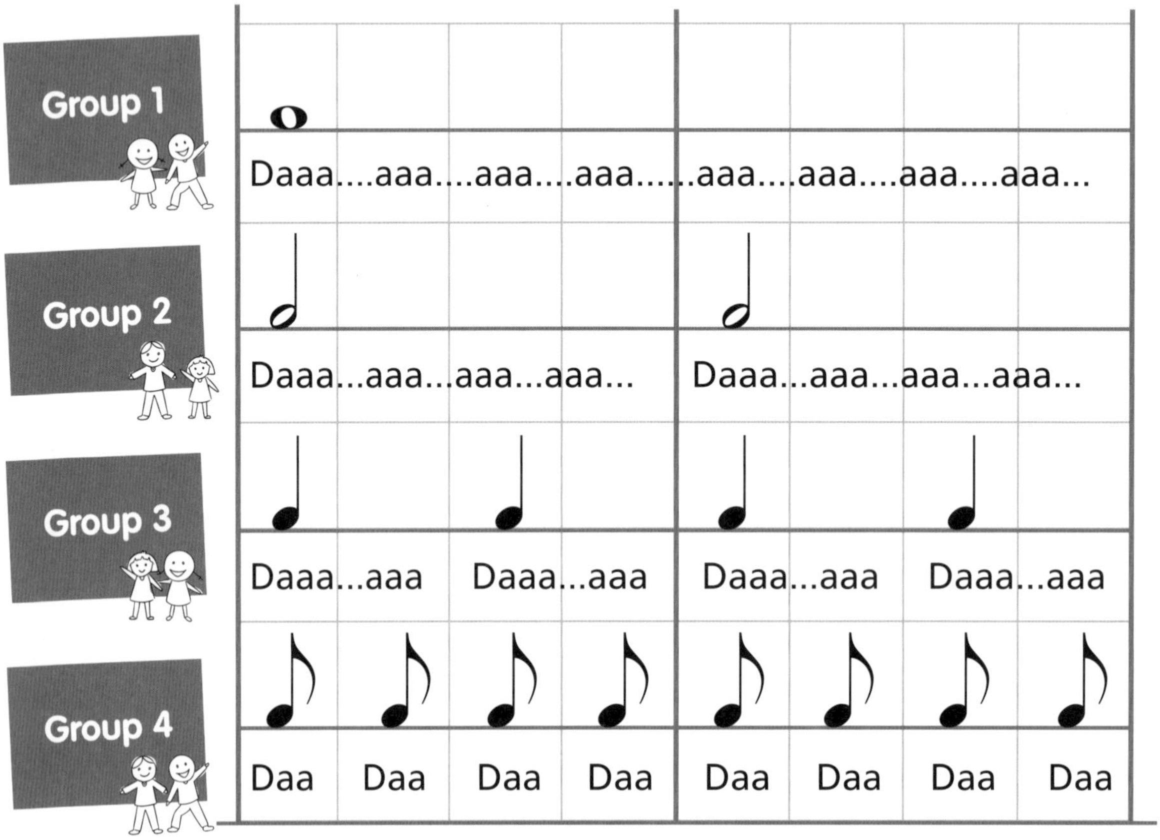

1. ________________ is the longest note.

2. There are two ________________ in one 𝅝 .

3. One 𝅗𝅥 is twice as long as ________________ .

4. There are two ♪ in one ________________ .

5. One 𝅝 is made up of two ________________ and four ________________ .

Quick Reference

- 𝅝 whole note
- 𝅗𝅥 half note
- ♩ quarter note
- ♪ eighth note

Name: Date:

The Notes and Rests

Materials:

- *Old MacDonald* song sheet (with notes)
- *Row Your Boat* and other nursery rhymes or familiar song sheets

Singing Out

Motivation:

To sing expressively and convey the meaning of the text with changes in volume or speed and substitute different words in familiar songs or create new verses

What to Do:

1. Hand out the song sheets and notice that we can "see" the song by looking at its notes and rests.

2. Clap out the rhythm of each song together.

3. Have the students sit or stand up tall. Have everyone make a low "hum" and notice where this sound is coming from – the chest. Have them slowly try to reach a higher note, noticing where the sound is moving.

4. Encourage clarity by having them "spend" air from the diaphragm and pronounce vowels and consonants clearly. The tongue should be relaxed and in a forward position, just below the lower teeth.

5. Sing these and other songs together. Change the speed, volume, and expression to alter the effect of the song. (e.g. Sing *Old MacDonald* as a sad song, or sing *Row Your Boat* very slowly and then very quickly).

6. Introduce the idea that *Old MacDonald* no longer has a farm but a town. Re-write the verses together.

Variation:

Have the students rewrite the verses of *Row Your Boat* or any other familiar song or nursery rhyme (e.g. Jump, Jump, Jump the Rope).

Name: Date:

Where the Symbols Go

Objective: *To recognize that the treble clef defines the names of the lines and spaces on the staff, to understand that specific pitches may be represented by notes, and to learn the definition of unison*

We know how long to play or rest, but how do we know what SOUND notes make?

The special place that these notes and rest symbols sit is called a **staff**. The **treble clef** is the most common clef and is also known as the G clef. It looks a little bit like a cello.

Pitch is the highness or lowness of a note. Music is interesting because the pitch can vary. If you add a change in pitch to a rhythm and beat, you have a song. We see changes in pitch by how notes are placed on the staff.

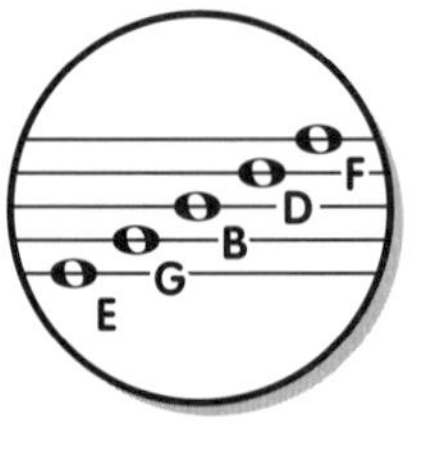

The lines (and notes) on the treble clef staff are named **E G B D F**. An easy trick to remember these lines or notes is with the saying "**E**very **G**ood **B**oy **D**oes **F**ine."

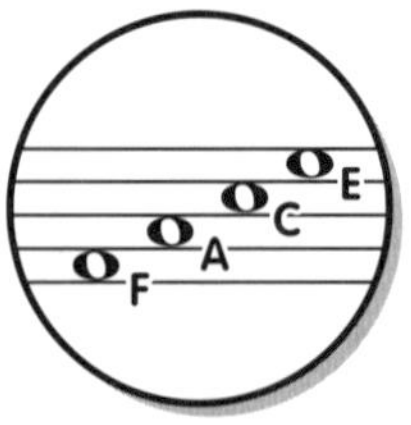

The spaces between these lines on the treble clef spell the word **F A C E**.

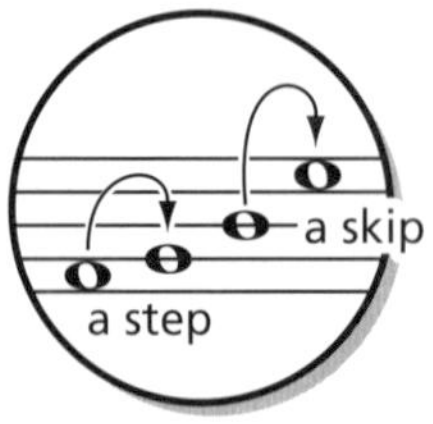

A **step** is when the notes change from a line to the next space or vice versa. A **skip** is any interval larger than a step. It is easier to read music when you notice whether the next note is a skip or a step from the last one.

When two notes on the same line or in the same space are sung or played simultaneously, it is called **unison**.

Name: Date:

Where the Symbols Go

A. Cut and paste the clef and notes in the correct boxes.

treble clef | E | F | G | A | B | C | D | E | F

B. Name the notes.

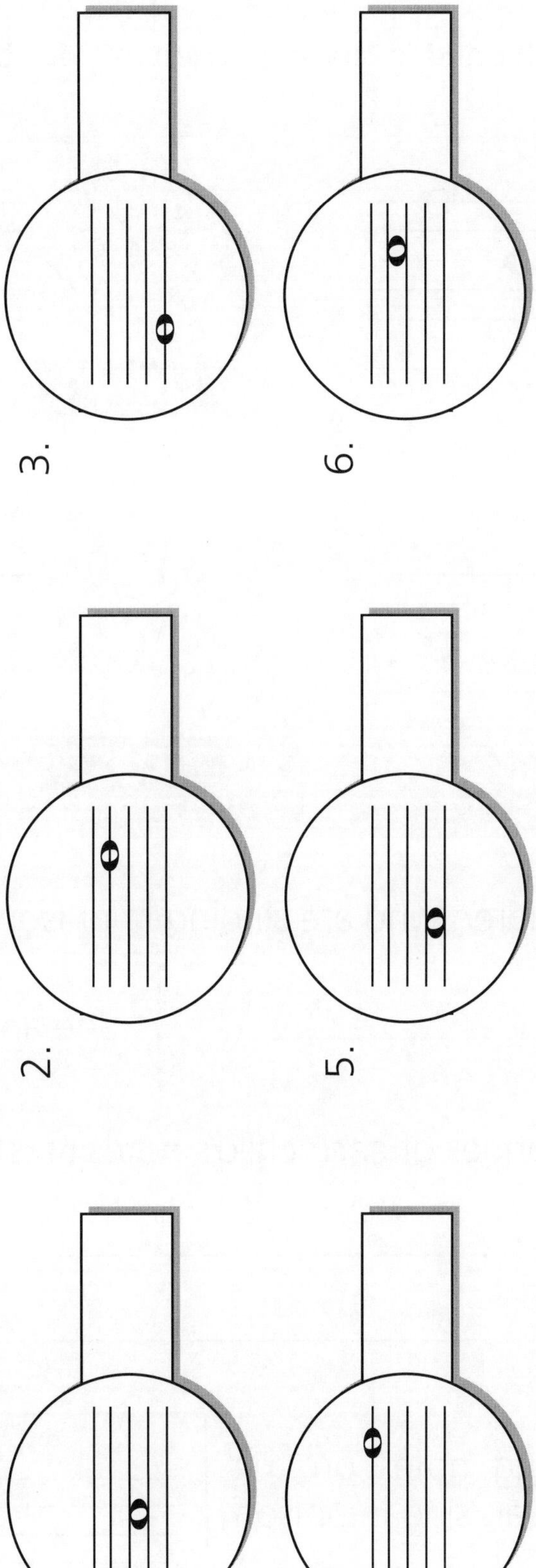

1. 2. 3. 4. 5. 6.

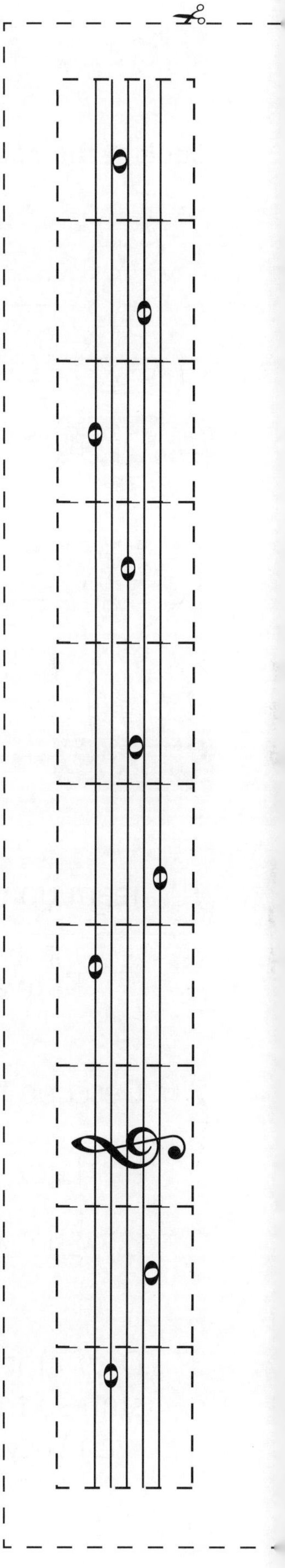

Name: Date:

Where the Symbols Go

Look at the notes each child is singing. Then answer the questions.

1. Team up the children who are singing in unison.

   Kate and ____________________ | Joe and ____________________

2. Describe the changes of each child's notes (in steps/in skips).

   a. Lucy ____________________

   b. Eric ____________________

3. Draw the missing notes on the staff so that Jill can sing in unison with Lucy.

Name: Date:

Where the Symbols Go

Materials:

- blank paper
- pencils
- familiar recorded music of teacher's choice

Mapping the Melody

Motivation:

To create melodic contour "maps" that indicate the direction of pitch (higher and lower) in familiar songs

What to Do:

1. Define a melodic contour map as a way of showing the direction of pitch in a song to show its melody.
2. Have the children sing *Twinkle, Twinkle Little Star* together, tapping on their desks or tables to the beat.
3. Start again, and this time sing slower and have them do a "thumbs up" if they think the pitch or notes are going higher or "thumbs down" if it's going lower.
4. Sing the song again, this time making marks on the page, showing higher or lower pitch. They can do this with lines (like a heart monitor), "x"s, or circles. Trade with a partner and see if he or she is able to recognize the song using the contour map.
5. Make melodic contour maps together and independently for other familiar music.
6. Out of the familiar music played, have each student choose one song to map out. Again, trade with a partner to see if he or she can guess the song.

Variation:

Have the students make the maps with paint or bingo stampers. If the weather is nice, and you have a portable music player, go outside and make line maps along the sidewalk with chalk.

Listening to Music

Objective: *To communicate thoughts and feelings about music and use appropriate musical terminology to describe specific songs*

Music fills our lives. Infants are lulled to sleep with quiet melodies. Toddlers wait, wide-eyed with wonder for "POP, goes the weasel!" Teenagers seem attached to IPods and MP3 players. Some are moved by the symphony and others by rock concerts. We need music for the way it makes us feel and how it expresses what our own words cannot say.

Music can make us feel energetic or alive. It can melt a hard heart or stir up anger. Music can bring on a feeling of fatigue and lull one to sleep. The mood created in a piece of music can cause listeners to be swept away.

Listen to these pieces and see what feeling or mood is created by their different tone colours (specific sounds of individual instruments or voices), tempo, dynamics, and rhythm.

- Beethoven's *Moonlight Sonata*
- *Let It Be* by The Beatles
- *Blowing in the Wind* by Bob Dylan
- *Dance of the Sugar Plum Fairies* by Tchaikovsky
- *Hush Little Baby*

How do they make you feel? Which songs do you like? What makes one your favourite? Is it its tempo (speed), dynamics (volume), or range in pitch?

Suppose you have to pick the "best" song in a music contest. Which will you choose, and why? Write it down in your journal.

Name: Date:

Listening to Music

Listen to the pieces of music. Describe their tempos, dynamics, and tone colours. Check the circles or write your own descriptions.

Wheels on the Bus

Tempo	Dynamics	Tone Colour		
○ slow	○ quiet	○ mellow	○ rich	○ whispering
○ moderate	○ mid	○ resonant	○ dull	○ light
○ fast	○ loud	○ piercing	○ muted	○ ________

My Bonnie Lies over the Ocean

Tempo	Dynamics	Tone Colour		
○ slow	○ quiet	○ mellow	○ rich	○ whispering
○ moderate	○ mid	○ resonant	○ dull	○ light
○ fast	○ loud	○ piercing	○ muted	○ ________

Jingle Bells

Tempo	Dynamics	Tone Colour		
○ slow	○ quiet	○ mellow	○ rich	○ whispering
○ moderate	○ mid	○ resonant	○ dull	○ light
○ fast	○ loud	○ piercing	○ muted	○ ________

Name: Date:

Listening to Music

A. Hum the music of each song. Then write how you feel.

sad happy peaceful energetic
excited patriotic soothed loyal

1. *Amazing Grace* ____________
2. *BINGO* ____________
3. *Mary Had a Little Lamb* ____________
4. *The Ants Go Marching* ____________
5. *Five Little Monkeys* ____________
6. *Hush-a-Bye Baby* ____________
7. *O Canada* ____________
8. *Rain, Rain, Go Away* ____________

B. What is your favourite song/music? What mood does it create?

My Favourite Song/Music: ____________

Mood Created: ____________

Name: Date:

Listening to Music

Materials:

- *Hush-a-Bye Baby* song sheet (and recording)
- *Frère Jacques* song sheet (and recording)
- *Waltzing Matilda* song sheet (and recording)

Motivation:

To express a response to music from a variety of cultures and historical periods

What to Do:

1 Introduce the idea that people have sung music throughout history for many reasons. Music can evoke an endless variety of feelings and responses.

2 Play each song first and encourage the students to use their arms to "act out" the music. Discuss the different emotions evoked in these pieces.

3 Explain the historical significance of these pieces.

Hush-A-Bye-Baby

- written by a pilgrim from the Mayflower

A pilgrim noticed that native women rocked their babies from branches in trees.

Frère Jacques

(Are You Sleeping?)

- an old, traditional song

It is not known which brother – John or James – the song is referring to.

Waltzing Matilda

- written by Banjo Paterson in 1895 in Australia

The music is credited to Christina Macpherson. "Matilda" means old battle maid.

4 Hand out the song sheets, pointing out that the symbols help us sing the music.

5 Play each song, and sing along. Encourage expression.

Follow up:

Pick one song, and draw a picture of what you see when you hear it. Use colours to show the mood of the picture. Write how it makes you feel, and what it makes you think of, at the bottom of your page.

Name: Date:

The Orchestra Families

Objective: *To identify individual instruments of the woodwind, brass, string, and percussion families*

Instruments are grouped into families because they are related to one another. They often look alike, are made of the same types of materials, and make sound in the same way.

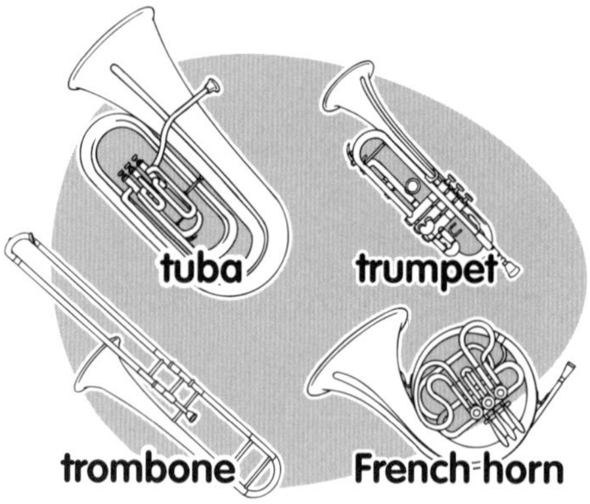

The **brass** family is made of brass. All instruments that belong to this family have a pipe-like centre that widens at the end like a bell. To create sound with one of these instruments, you make a buzzing noise into the special mouthpiece. Valves on the pipes can be pressed to change the pitch.

The **string** family is comprised of instruments mostly made of wood. Their hollowed bodies allow sound to vibrate. A bow, made with real horse-tail hair, is sometimes moved across the strings to create sound. Other times, a musician will use his or her fingers to pluck or hit the strings.

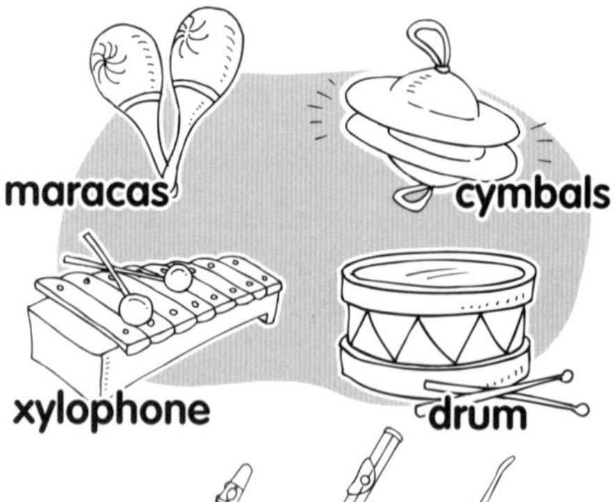

The **percussion** family is made up of instruments that you can hit, scrape, or shake! Some of these can play a change in pitch, and others play the rhythm or beat.

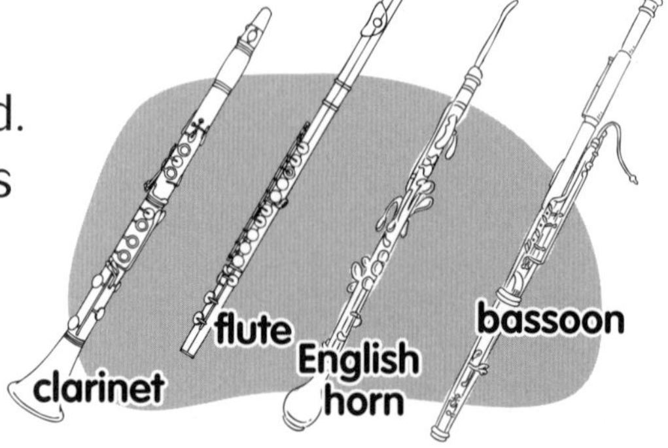

The **woodwind** family can also be made of wood. These instruments are narrow pipes with holes along them. A musician blows out through the mouthpiece and uses his or her fingers to cover the holes, which changes the pitch.

Name: Date:

The Orchestra Families

Cut and paste to complete the picture of each instrument. Then decide which family it belongs to. Write "brass", "string", "woodwind", or "percussion".

French Horn

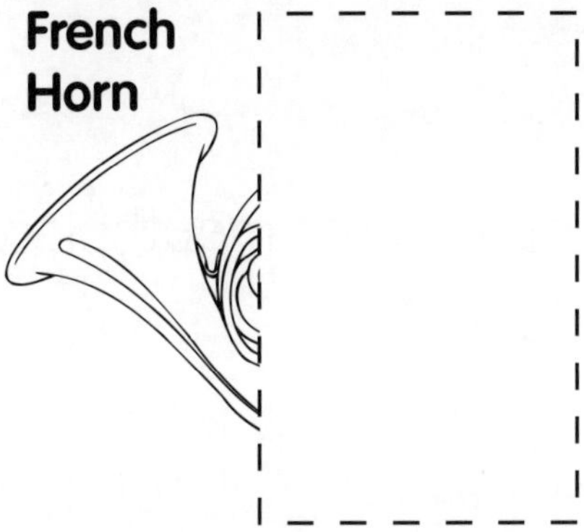

____

Cello

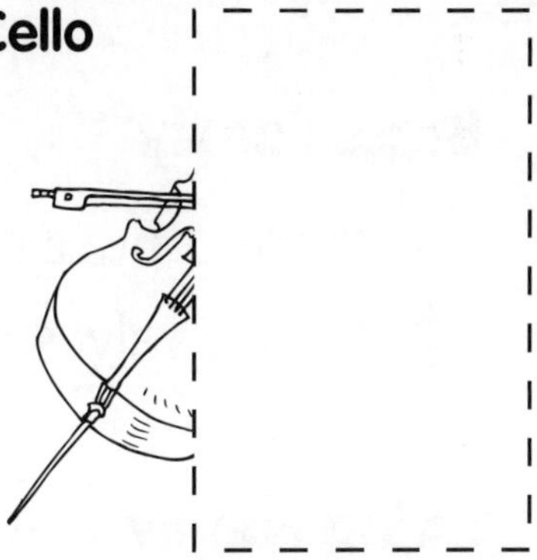

____

Clarinet

____

English Horn

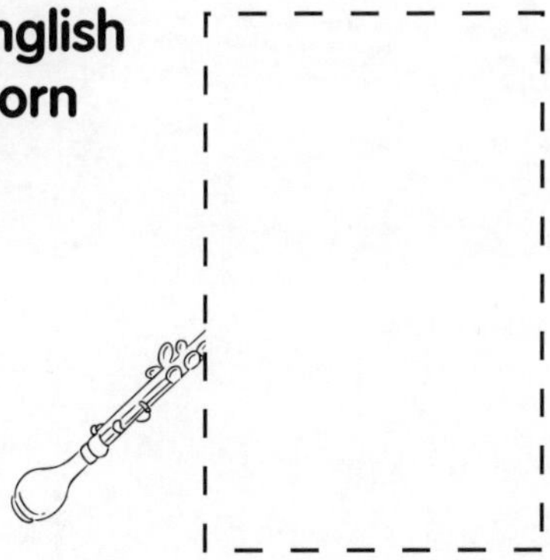

____

Timpani

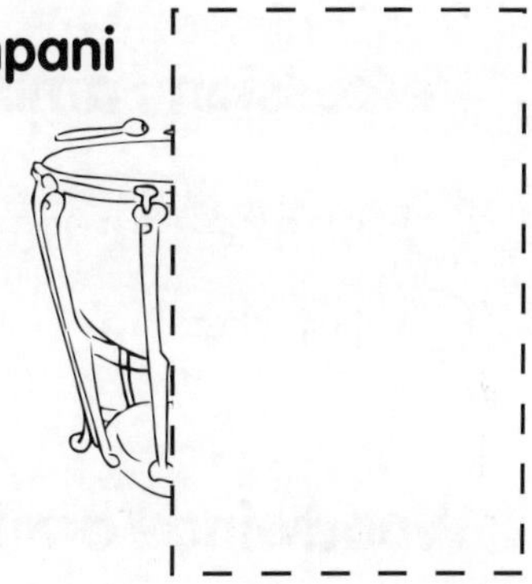

____

Castanets

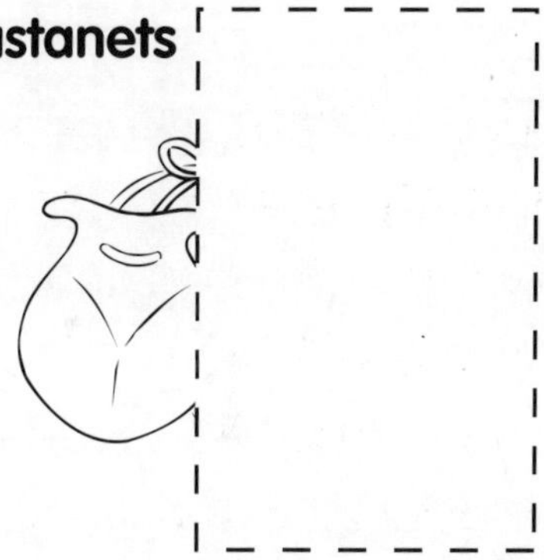

____

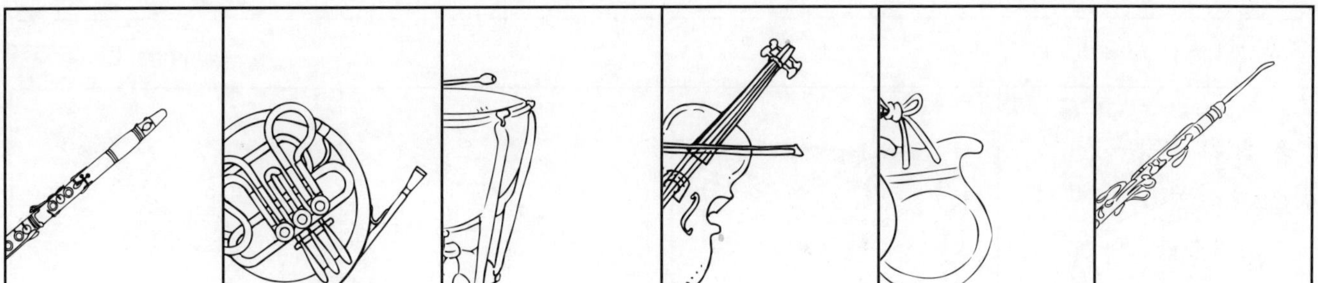

Name: Date:

The Orchestra Families

Cut and paste the instrument that belongs to each family. Then check the statement(s) that correctly describes how the particular instrument below makes sound.

1.

Brass Family

- ○ make a buzzing sound into the mouthpiece
- ○ hit the valves on the pipes

2.

String Family

- ○ move a bow across the strings
- ○ use fingers to pluck the strings

3.

Percussion Family

- ○ shake the bars
- ○ hit the bars with mallets

4.

Woodwind Family

- ○ blow air through the mouthpiece
- ○ blow air through the holes

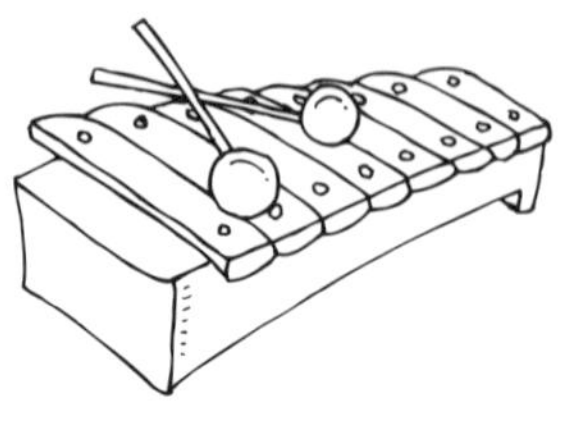

Name: Date:

The Orchestra Families

Materials:

- shoe box (with lid)
- rubber bands of various thicknesses
- two unsharpened pencils
- tape and scissors
- pencil and compass

Motivation:

To make our own instruments with handy materials

What to Do:

1 Draw a circle in the middle of the lid with a compass.

2 Cut out the circle carefully to make a hole in the lid.

3 Put the lid back on the shoe box and secure a pencil at each end of the box with tape.

4 Stretch several rubber bands around the box.

Variation:

Wrap the "guitar" with aluminum foil and secure a paper towel roll on the side with tape to make it look more like a real guitar.

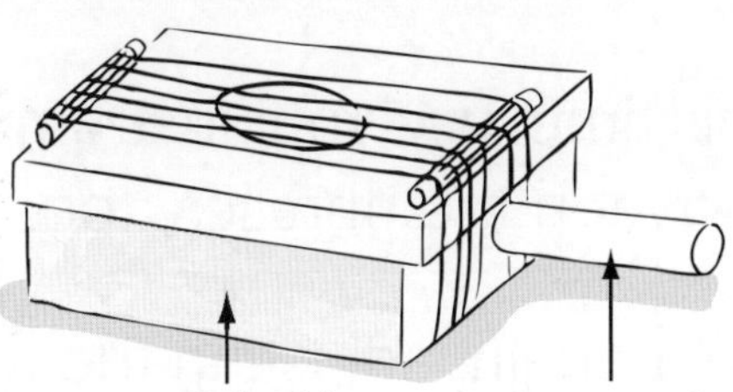

Name: Date:

Making Music

Objective: *To create an accompaniment for a story, poem, or drama presentation using knowledge of beat, rhythm, and tone colour*

Now that you have your own instrument, you can put it to great use! Let's remember the elements of music:

Your instrument might plunk, honk, clang, or toot. You might be able to create a melody. Perhaps you'll carry a rhythm of a *plink, plink, plinkety plink*.

Read this together with expression, noticing the beat. Pause between phrases and consider how the instrument can be used for this rhyme:

Old Man Moses

Old Man Moses, sick in bed,
He called the doctor, the doctor said,
"Take two steps forward and turn yourself around.
Do the wiggle waggle and get out of town!"

This time, use your instrument to create an accompaniment. Add some music between the phrases, too. Which parts will be faster or louder?

Do it again, adjusting the tempo and dynamics.

Name: Date:

Making Music

Answer the questions to explain how to create different effects with the instruments.

1. **Guitar**

Increase tempo

- ◯ pluck strings faster
- ◯ pluck strings harder
- ◯ pluck strings more slowly

Increase dynamics

- ◯ pluck strings more slowly
- ◯ pluck strings harder
- ◯ pluck strings lightly

2. **Flute**

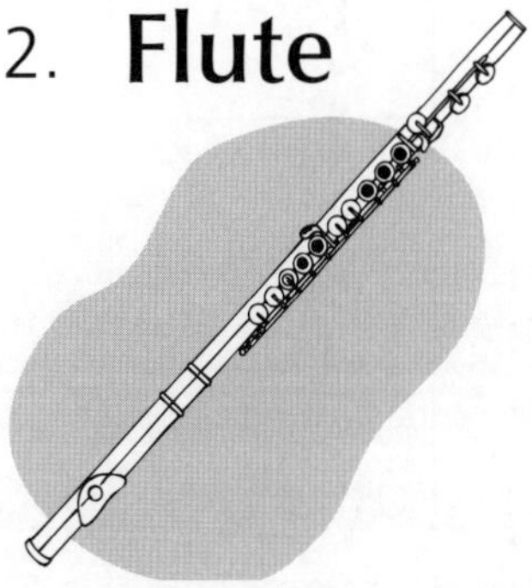

Decrease dynamics

- ◯ blow less air
- ◯ blow more air
- ◯ cover fewer holes

Change pitch

- ◯ blow air lightly
- ◯ cover different holes
- ◯ blow air harder

3. a. *How would you make the tempo slower?*

____

____

b. Can we change pitch with this drum?

____

Name: Date:

Making Music

Read the rhyme with the class. Then decide which instruments you want to play to create an accompaniment for each set.

Hot Cross Buns

Set 1	Set 2	
		Hot cross buns! Hot cross buns!
		One a penny, two a penny – Hot cross buns
		If you have no daughters, give them to your sons
		One a penny, two a penny – Hot cross buns

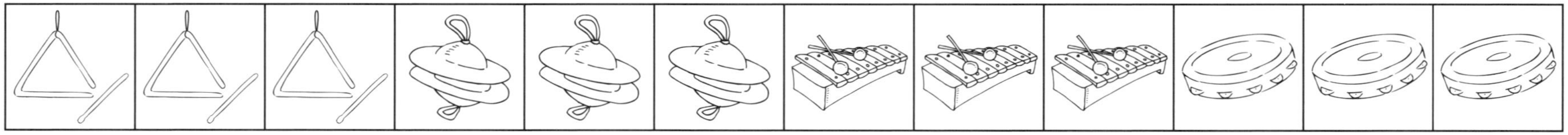

Name: Date:

Making Music

Musical Composition

Materials:

- triangle
- cymbals
- xylophone
- tambourine
- hand-made instruments

Motivation:

To create musical compositions that show appropriate use of some of the elements of music

What to Do:

1 Listen to *The Sorcerer's Apprentice* by Dukas. Discuss how Dukas uses tempo, dynamics, and tone colour to create a mood.

- What did this music make you think of?
- How did it make you feel?
- Which parts did you like best?

2 Experiment with the instruments. Can the sound be adjusted to create a mood?

3 Read the following verse and create an accompaniment for it. Pay attention to the beat, rhythm, tempo, and dynamics. Some lines may be more effective with only certain instruments:

In a cabin
In the woods
A little man by the window stood
Saw a rabbit
Hopping by
Knocking on the door as hard as he could
"HELP ME! HELP ME!" the rabbit cried
"Before the hunter shoots my hide!"
Come little rabbit, come inside
Safe with me you can abide.

Art Lessons Grades 3-4

Visual Arts

Name: Date:

Warm Colours

Objective: *To recognize the warm colours (red, orange, and yellow)*

How do you feel when you think of a campfire or a ray of sunshine through the trees?

How do you feel when you see a sunset?

What colours come to mind when you think of heat?

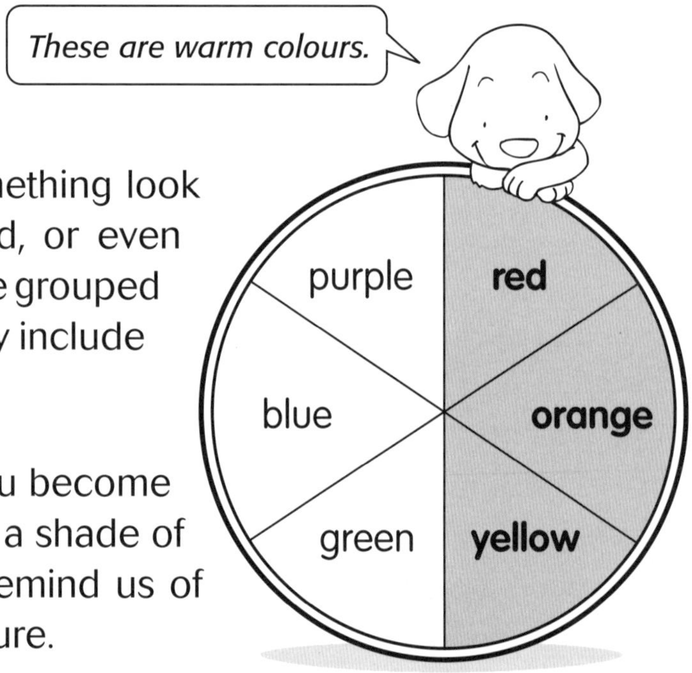

Artists can use colour to make something look real, express emotion, create mood, or even show temperature. Warm colours are grouped on one side of the colour wheel; they include **red**, **orange**, and **yellow**.

Think about what happens when you become embarrassed. Does your face turn a shade of red? Reds, oranges, and yellows remind us of fire, sunlight, and a rise in temperature.

Colours can influence our emotions. Warm colours can make us feel enthusiastic and energetic. It is believed that they can slightly increase our circulation and body temperature, making us feel warmer.

Warm colours give the impression of moving toward the viewer. An image that is red, orange, or yellow might seem closer than one that is blue or green. An artist can use warm colours to make something stand out on the page.

Name: Date:

Warm Colours

A. Name the warm colours. Then circle the correct answers.

Warm colours: ______________ , ______________ , and ______________

Characteristics of Warm Colours:

1. They suggest warmth / cold .
2. They make us think of fire / shadow and a fall / rise in temperature.
3. They also make us feel isolated / enthusiastic and energetic.
4. They appear to move away from / toward the viewer.
5. They are able to make something disappear / stand out on the page.

B. Colour the gift boxes green. Then colour the hearts in the boxes red, blue, and purple. Which heart stands out on the page?

Name: Date:

Warm Colours

Colour the pictures and answer the question.

1. Colour the house on the left red and the one on the right green.

Which house seems to be warmer? ____________

2. Colour the pots at different temperatures with the given colours.

red
yellow
blue
orange

Name: Date:

Warm Colours

Materials:

- 8.5 x 11″ paper
- red, orange, and yellow tempera paint
- paintbrush
- water
- 8.5 x 11″ black construction paper
- mixing tray

Motivation:

To create a sunset silhouette using the warm colours – red, orange, and yellow

What to Do:

1. Consider what a sunset looks like. The colours blend together beautifully. Use a small amount of red paint, mixed with water, to make a line near the top of the paper.

2. Encourage the students to mix the paint on the tray first to create their desired colours. Gradually add orange, and then yellow, continuing to make gentle, wavy, overlapping lines. The bottom third of the picture can be pure yellow mixed with water.

3. Use a small amount of water to blend the colours throughout the painting. Reddish-orange clouds can be added at the end, if desired.

4. Leave this to dry.

5. Draw the outline of landscape, such as an African safari, Arizona cacti, boats out to sea with a lighthouse, or a cityscape, on the black construction paper. Then cut and paste it to the front of the dry painting.

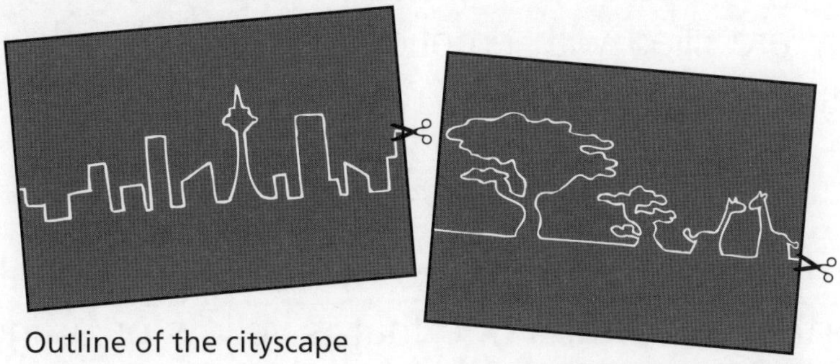

Outline of the cityscape

Outline of the African safari

Tip:

Use a wet rag or sponge to spread the paint.

Name: Date:

Cool Colours

Objective: *To recognize the cool colours (blue, green, and purple)*

What colours come to mind when you think of a deep, cold ocean?

How do you feel when you see a frozen lake surrounded by fresh, snow-covered evergreens?

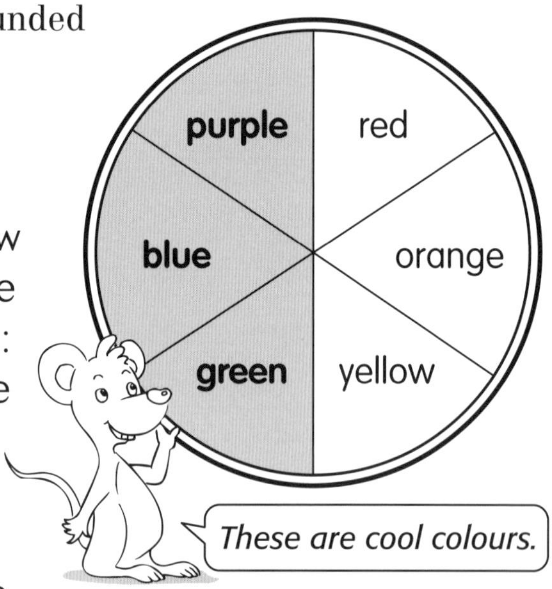

Now that we have seen how artists show temperature with warm colours, we can take a look at the other side of the colour wheel: **blue**, **green**, and **purple**, known as the cool colours.

Cool colours can make us feel calm. An artist might choose these colours to soothe the viewer, resulting in a peaceful or relaxed response or mood.

Artists also use these colours to show feelings and create a mood. In Vincent Van Gogh's famous painting, *The Starry Night*, the swirling blue brushstrokes in the sky are filled with emotion. The quiet town and the peaceful church rest silently in the distance.

The Starry Night
Vincent Van Gogh, 1889

Cool colours appear to move away from the viewer. An image that is blue or purple might seem farther away than one that is yellow or orange. An artist can use cool colours to make something move back on the page.

Name: Date:

Cool Colours

Answer the questions.

1. Colour each circle with a cool colour. Then name the cool colour.

2. Colour the walls in the top picture blue and those in the bottom picture orange. Then look at the pictures from a distance.

Which table seems to be farther from you? ____________________

Name: Date:

Cool Colours

Maggie wants to make a card for her friend who is sick. Colour the card with cool colours to show your sympathy. Then cut it out and add your own personal get-well wish.

Name: Date:

Cool Colours

Materials:

- 8.5 x 11″ paper
- mixing tray
- sponge
- water
- tinfoil
- permanent felt-tip pens (red, orange, and yellow)
- vegetable netting (as found on mandarin orange boxes)
- blue, purple, and green tempera paint

Motivation:

To create an ocean scene using cool colours to demonstrate how colour can influence the viewer's emotions

What to Do:

1. Mix the cool colours on the tray.
2. Use the moist sponge to drag the paint in "waves" across the paper. Gradually add a variety of blues, purples, and greens to add interest, making waves with overlapping lines.
3. Use the sponge to dab the blue paint on the paper, creating the impression of splashing water. Then leave the paper to dry.
4. Draw a simple fish, approximately 5 cm long on the tinfoil.
5. Use the pens to colour the fish. You can put a thick stripe of red down the back, followed with orange and yellow (much like a sunset). Make several more fish.
6. Tape the piece of tinfoil to the vegetable netting, and gently rub your thumbnail on the foil to produce the texture of scales.
7. Cut out the fish and paste them to the ocean background.

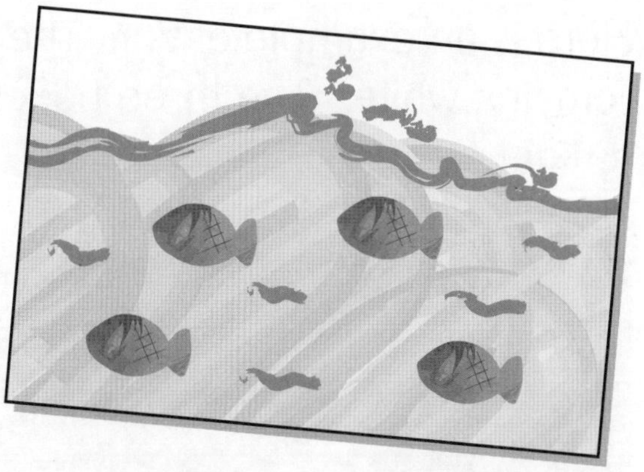

Follow up:

Discuss how the colours make the water look like the background. Do the fish, being warmer colours, stand out? How does this picture make you feel? Write a journal entry about the mood created by the picture.

Name: Date:

Monochromatic Colours – Tints

Objective: *To identify monochromatic colour schemes (tints of one colour)*

Everyone has a favourite colour. If yours is red, what kind of red is it? Imagine the vast variety of reds. Consider the "red" of an apple; is it the same as the red of a stop light or sunset? When artists use a colour, they can alter it by changing its lightness or darkness, known as **value**.

Monochrome means **"one colour"**. To create a lighter value of a colour, such as blue, you add white. Each time you add more white, the value changes. The resulting colours are called **tints**. The lightest value is pure white; the darkest is black.

In a painting or drawing, artists will use different colour values to make things look more realistic, create a mood, or express a feeling. A picture can be more subtle or peaceful when the contrast between colours is minimal.

Value also creates depth in a picture, making a form look three dimensional with highlights (tints).

Here is an example of tint. The first box is a pure colour. The box at the end remains white. The three boxes between show a gradual change from dark to light.

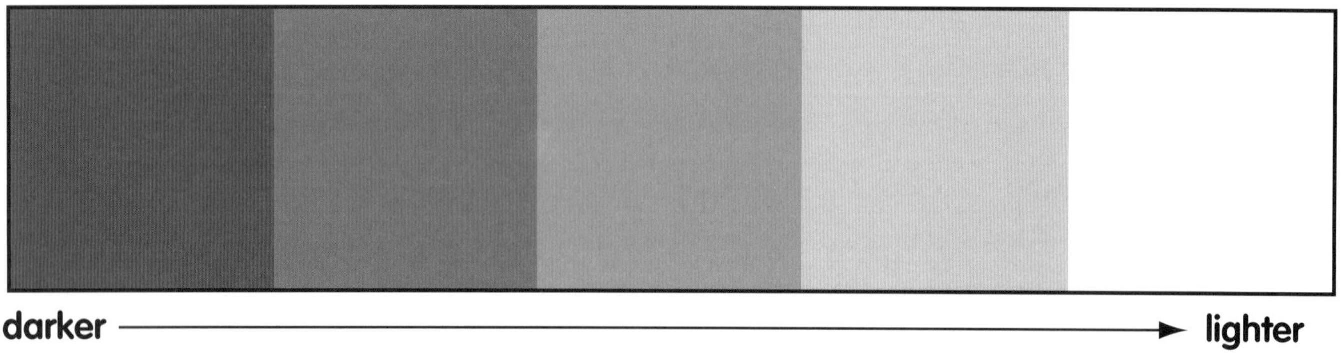

Name: Date:

Monochromatic Colours – Tints

Colour the first box in each row with the specified colour. Then colour the other three boxes showing a gradual change from dark to light by adding white to the colours. Leave the last box white.

red

blue

green

orange

Name: Date:

Monochromatic Colours – Tints

Colour the boxes to show a gradual change from solid blue to white. Then colour the labelled parts of each figure with the matching colours to create a three-dimensional figure.

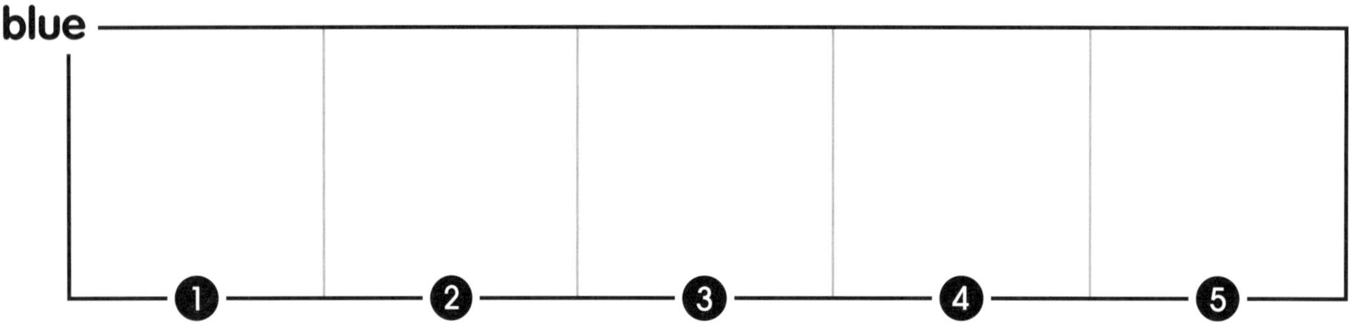

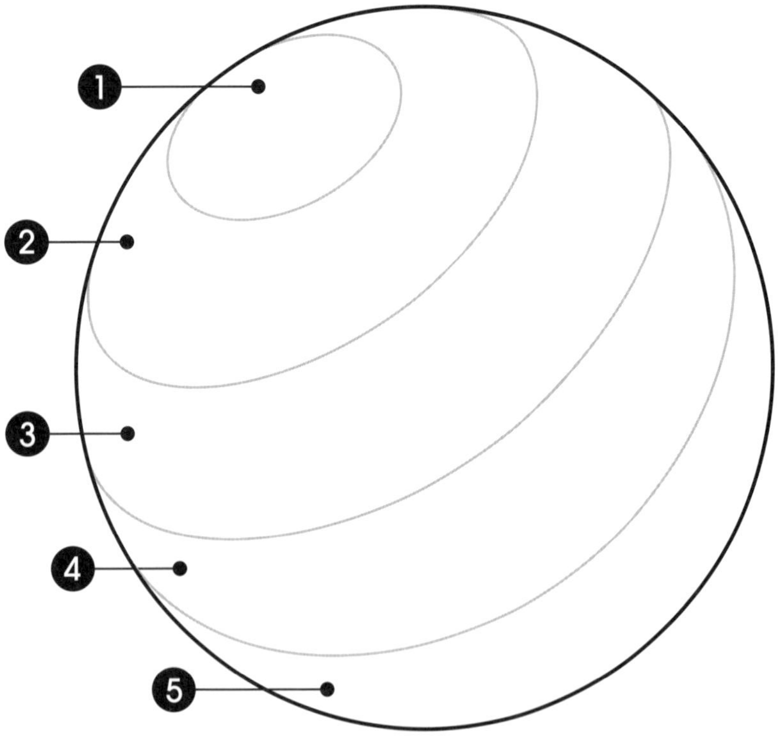

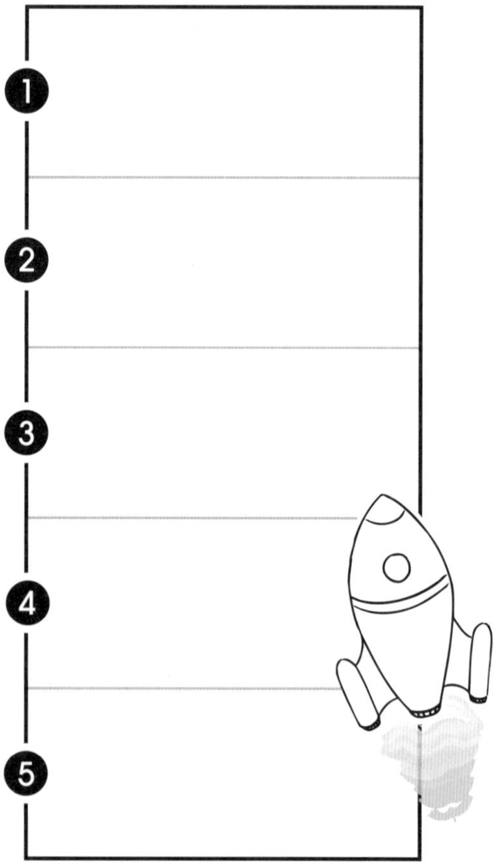

Name: Date:

Monochromatic Colours – Tints

Abstract Painting

Motivation:

To recognize the value of tints and that adding white to a colour changes its tint

Materials:

- permanent black marker
- cookie cutter with an interesting shape for tracing
- ruler
- tempera paint (one colour of choice and white)
- paintbrush
- water
- scrap paper
- paint tray for mixing

What to Do:

1 Place the cookie cutter on the scrap paper. Trace it several times with the black marker, varying its position and overlapping it.

2 Use the ruler to make five lines diagonally across the page, three in one direction and two in the other.

3 Have the students start with the pure colour, adding white gradually to experiment with different values on the scrap paper.

4 Have the students make four varying tints on the tray, each with enough paint to fill an area.

5 Paint the shapes with these tints, ensuring that the values close to each other are not too similar.

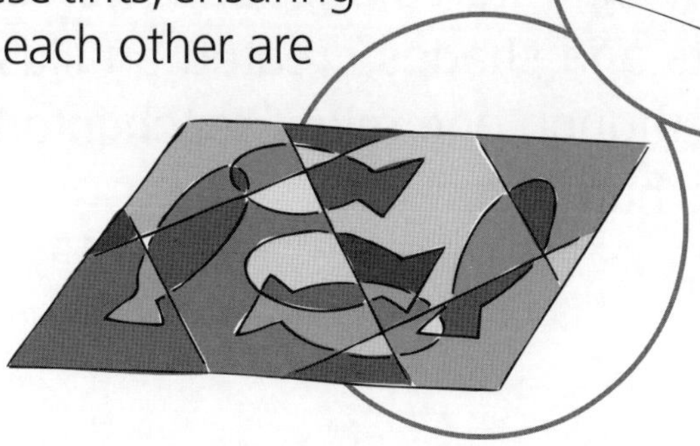

Picture of abstract art showing monochrome tints – 5 lines and several objects

Name: Date:

Monochromatic Colours – Shades

Objective: *To identify that monochromatic shades are made by adding black to a colour*

We have learned that tints are made when white is added to a pure colour. The white makes the colour lighter. In the same way, adding black to a colour can create darker values or **shades**.

Consider painting a picture of a golden retriever. What colours would you use? You may only need one colour with lighter and darker values (tints and shades). How would you paint a white rabbit? Could you add tiny amounts of black to the white paint to show shadows in its fur?

Artists use values to make images look real. If you were to use a pencil to draw three forms . . . a sphere, a cylinder and a cube, you could make them look three dimensional by gradually adding black. This technique is called **shading**. Lighter values are used for areas closest to the light, and darker values are used for the areas hidden from the light.

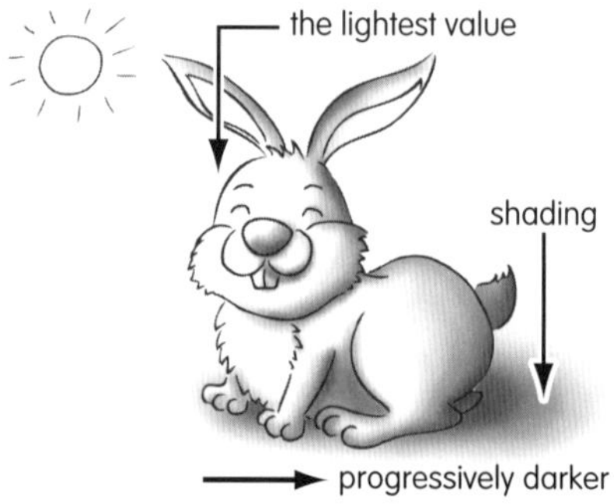

Albrecht Durer was a talented German artist, and he painted a monochromatic watercolour titled *The Young Hare*. His use of tints and shades created an illusory texture of fur. It is as though one might reach into the picture and touch the hare's soft fur.

The Young Hare
Albrecht Durer, 1502

Name: Date:

Monochromatic Colours – Shades

Check the pictures that have the correct shading.

1.

2.

3.

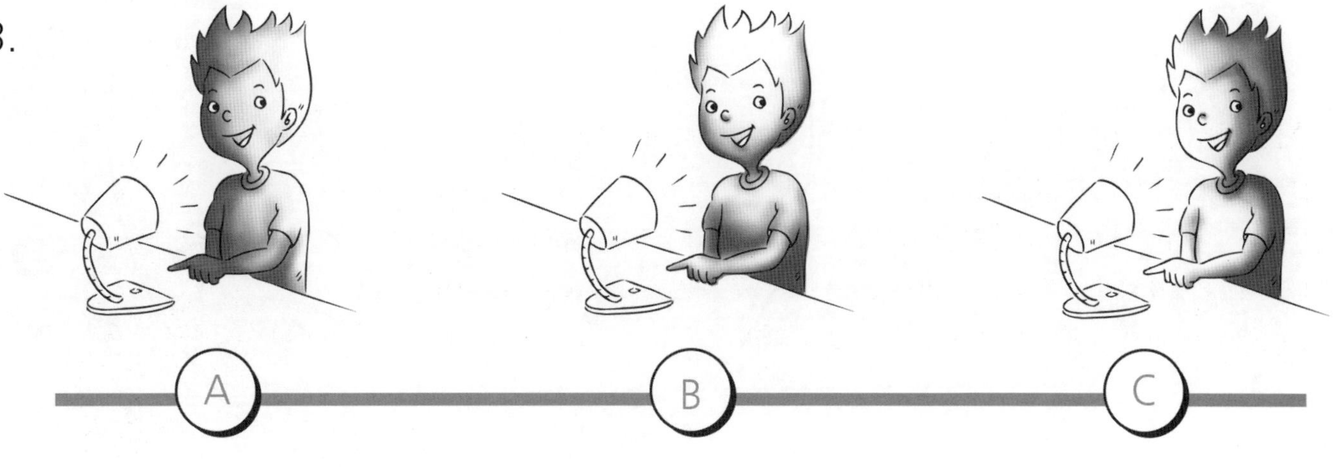

Name: Date:

Monochromatic Colours – Shades

Colour the boxes to show a gradual change from light blue to dark blue by adding tiny amounts of black. Then colour the labelled parts on the ball to show the shades.

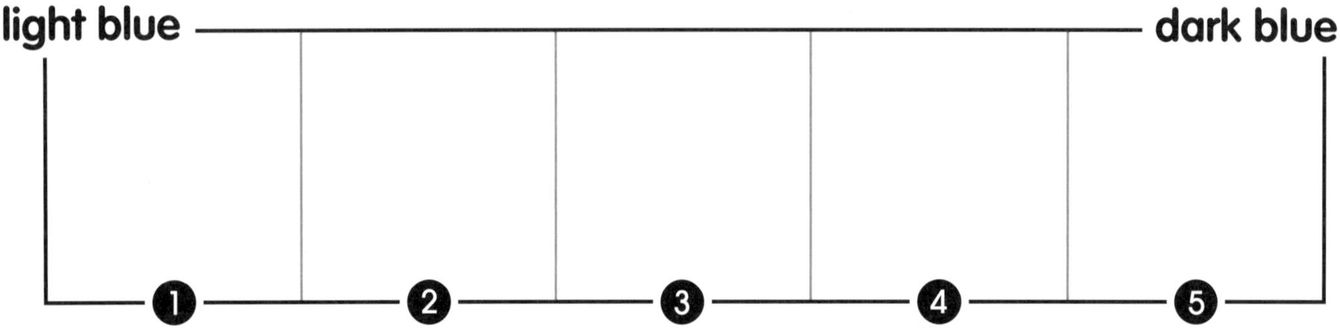

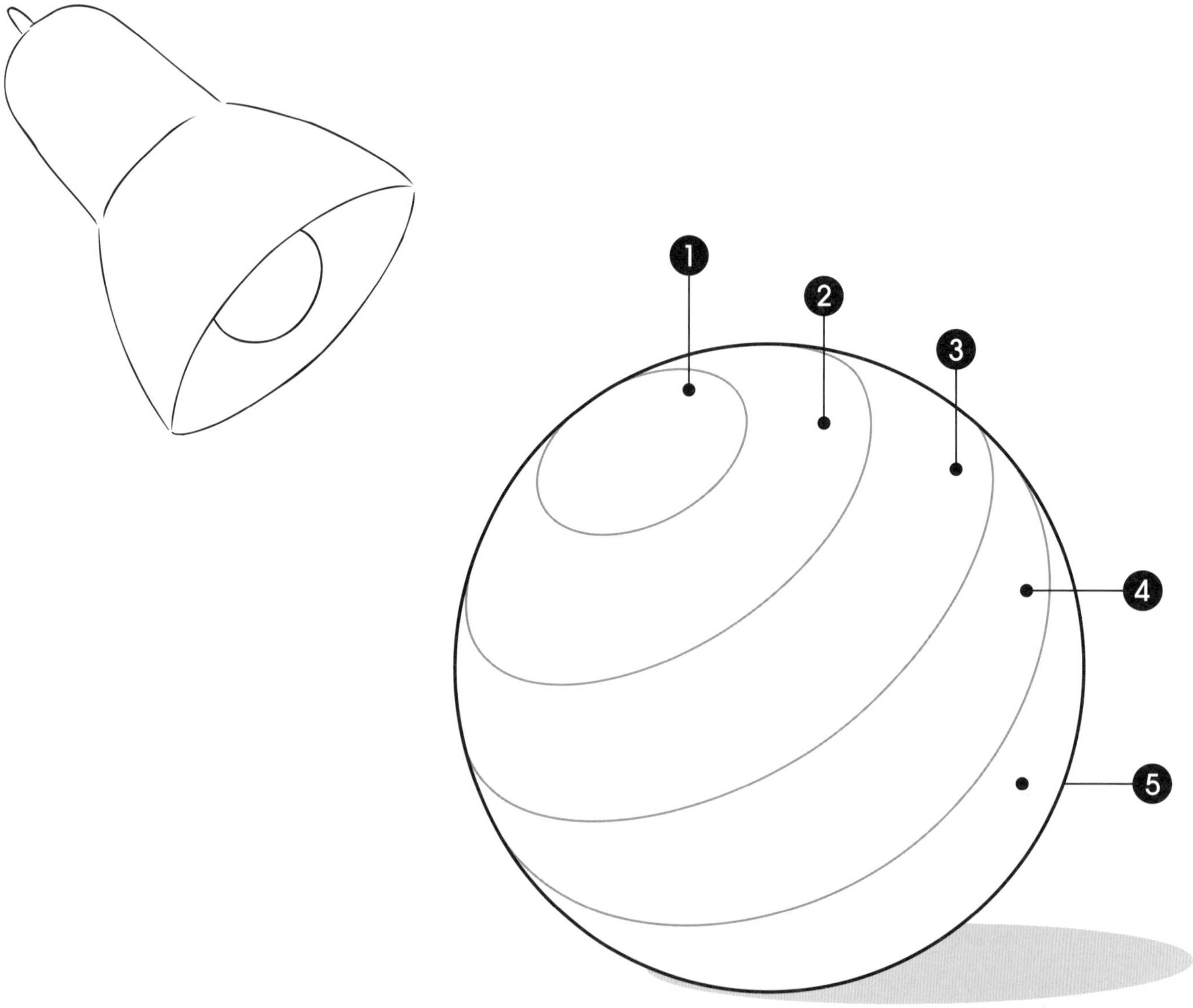

Name: Date:

Monochromatic Colours – Shades

Mosaic Image

Materials:

- magazine pictures of faces
- 9 x 12" white paper
- scissors
- glue stick
- large piece of construction paper
- white glue
- water

Motivation:

To create a mosaic of the face using various flesh tones

What to Do:

1. Cut up magazine pictures of faces, keeping similar tones together. Reserve one face for reference.
2. Choose shades that you can use to create the eyes, lips, nose, hair. Try to find a lot of different shades and tints of the same colour. (Darker flesh tones can be used for lips, eyebrows, hair, and the darkest ones can be used for the pupils, etc.) Outline the face on the paper.
3. Assemble and glue the squares in place creating the face, using the reserved magazine picture for reference.
4. When it is dry, paint over the whole image with white glue mixed with water. This will give it a glossy look.
5. Cut out the face, ensuring the edges are smooth, and mount it on to the construction paper or cardboard.

Variation:

Have the students bring in a close-up picture of themselves, and use it for reference to make a self-portrait.

Hint:

An excellent way to show shade and tint is to collect paint chips from the local paint store. The students can make a "value change" book with the chips, showing increasingly lighter tints or darker shades.

Name: Date:

Characteristics of Lines

Objective: *To identify the characteristics of a variety of lines (e.g. thick, thin, broken, dotted)*

When you make a mark on a piece of paper with a pencil, the first thing you will probably draw is a line. This line may be straight or curved, short or long, thick or thin, but it will always have at least one thing in common with all other lines.

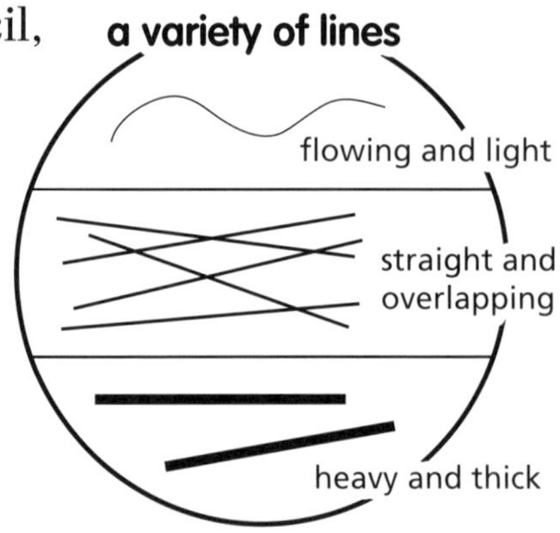

A **line** starts at a point (a single mark in space with an exact location) and extends from it.

Lines are one of the most basic elements of design. Artists use them to make shapes and forms, show movement, emotion, and ideas, and create mood.

What impression do these lines give you?

A child's first artistic expression in art is usually made of a variety of lines. Lines that are used to outline an image are called **contour lines**.

Lines come in all shapes and sizes. They can be different in their:

- **Length**

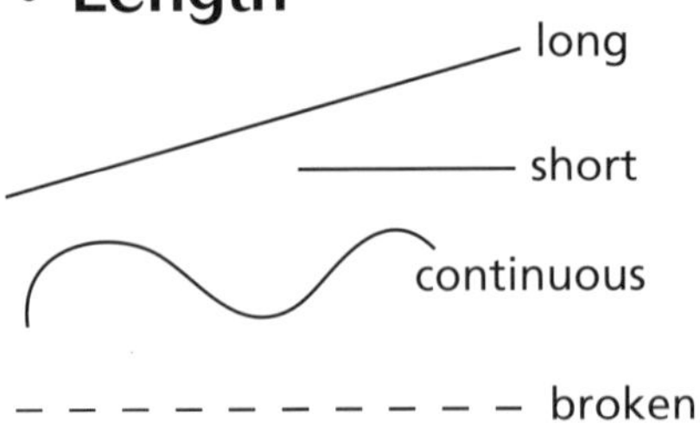

- **Width**

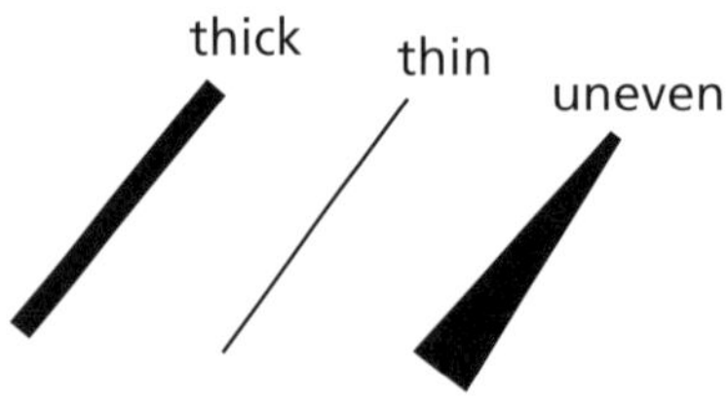

- **Direction**

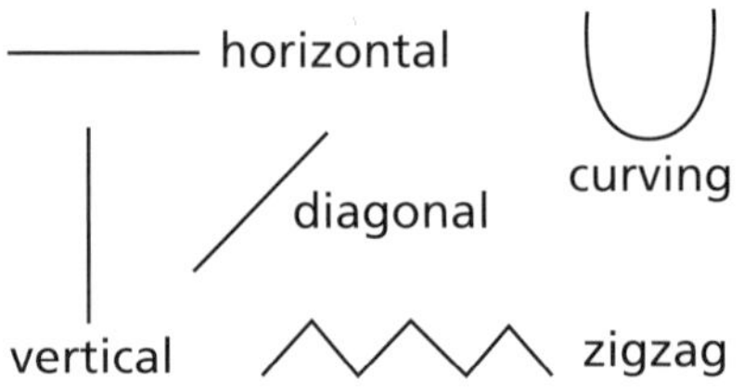

You can see lines everywhere around you: the curve of an arch, the straight lines of a skyscraper, and even the intricate veins of a leaf. Artists look for these lines so that they can capture how things really look and share their emotions or ideas.

Name: Date:

Characteristics of Lines

A. Which paintbrushes would be used to create the following lines? Match the paintbrushes with the correct lines. Then label the lines with the given description.

light heavy thin thick

B. Draw each type of line. Then write which line would be described as "happy" and which would be "angry".

light and curved	thick and zigzag
______________________	______________________

Name: Date:

Characteristics of Lines

Give three different characteristics of the lines in each image.

long short continuous broken thick thin uneven
horizontal vertical diagonal curving zigzag

1. 

____
____
____

2. 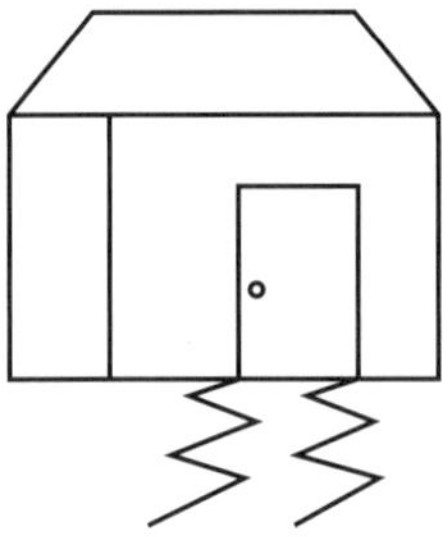

____
____
____

3. 

____
____
____

4. 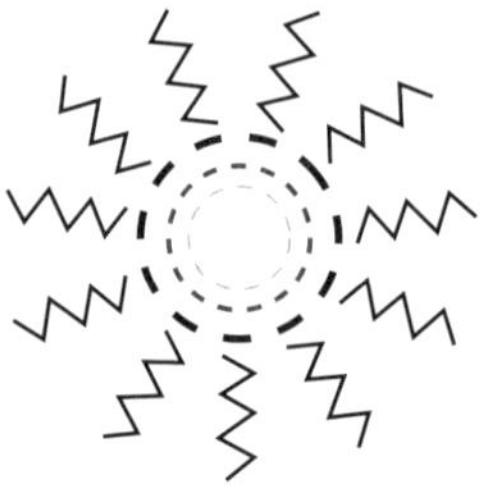

____
____
____

5. 

____
____
____

6. 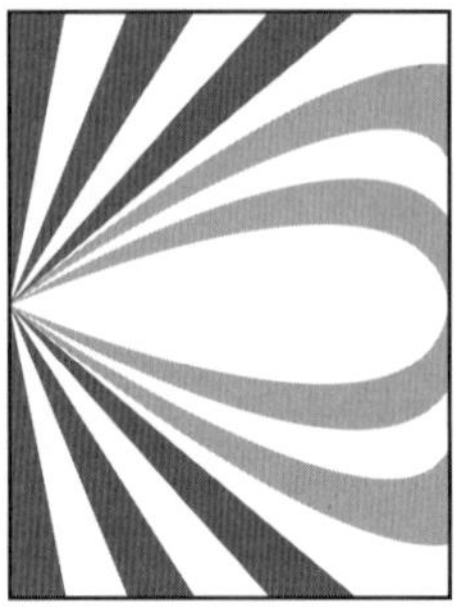

____
____
____

Name: Date:

Characteristics of Lines

A Moody Landscape

Materials:

- 9 x 12" paper
- marker – dark colour
- watercolour paint
- paintbrush
- water
- pencil
- tray

Motivation:

To experiment with a variety of lines to show emotion and movement

What to Do:

1. Draw a landscape in marker. Consider what will fill the landscape – trees, mountains, water, buildings, etc.

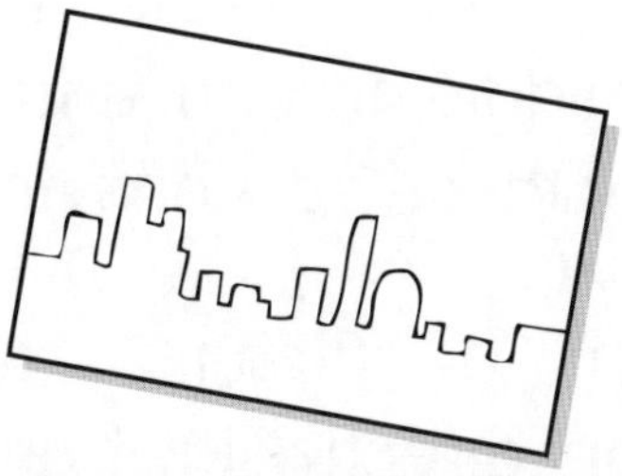

2. Draw lines with the markers to show the movement and feeling of the place. For example, have curvy lines show wind and dotted lines show sunshine. Have birds in the sky, spirals of wind across the sky, or a pattern of different trees. Try to fill the page with interesting and different lines.

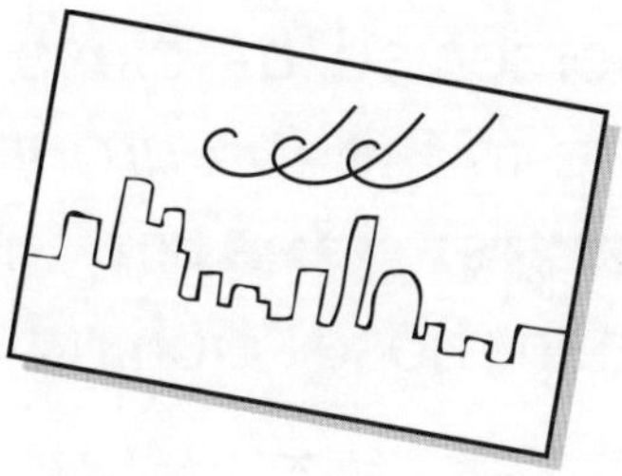

3. Add watercolour paint to fill in the images. Paint over the lines to blur them. Add new patterns with the paint to bring the picture to life.

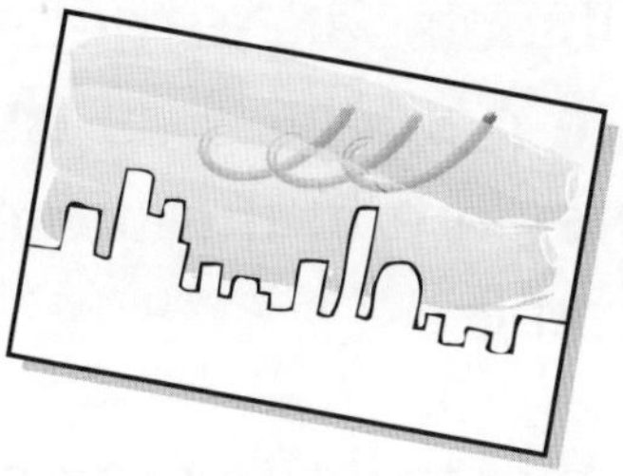

Tip:

Consider using warm or cool colours to create a particular mood. Think about the feeling and movement created by the lines while painting. Is it a stormy day? Is there excitement in the air? Is the wind calm or stirring something up?

Ask your friends how the painting makes them feel and what the different lines in the picture "say".

Name: Date:

Background, Middle Ground, and Foreground

Objective: *To label the background, middle ground, and foreground, and identify objects in each of these areas in a picture*

Looking out of your window, you will see that the world is framed like a picture. Can you see far into the horizon? Are there buildings or trees close by?

The space outside your window can be divided into three sections: background, middle ground, and foreground. Artists use this technique, or their awareness of these sections, to give their work depth.

In a picture, objects **low** or directly in front of us are perceived as closest to us and are in the *foreground*. They are **larger**, **clearer**, and **brighter** than those "behind" them.

Objects at a medium distance are perceived as **mid-ground**; they are in the the middle of the frame.

Objects farthest from us, in the *background*, are usually **higher** in the picture; they seem **less clear**, and their colours are **less intense** than those in both the foreground and middle ground.

The Group of Seven, a talented group of Canadian artists from the early 1900s, used great contrast between their back, middle, and foregrounds to show depth when painting the seasonal landscapes of Canada.

Name: Date:

Background, Middle Ground, and Foreground

Colour the area indicated for each picture.

background

middle ground

foreground

Name: Date:

Background, Middle Ground, and Foreground

Look at the size and detail of the images in the circles. Decide if the image belongs in the background, middle ground, or foreground of the pictures. Cut out the circles and glue them in their correct places. Then colour the pictures.

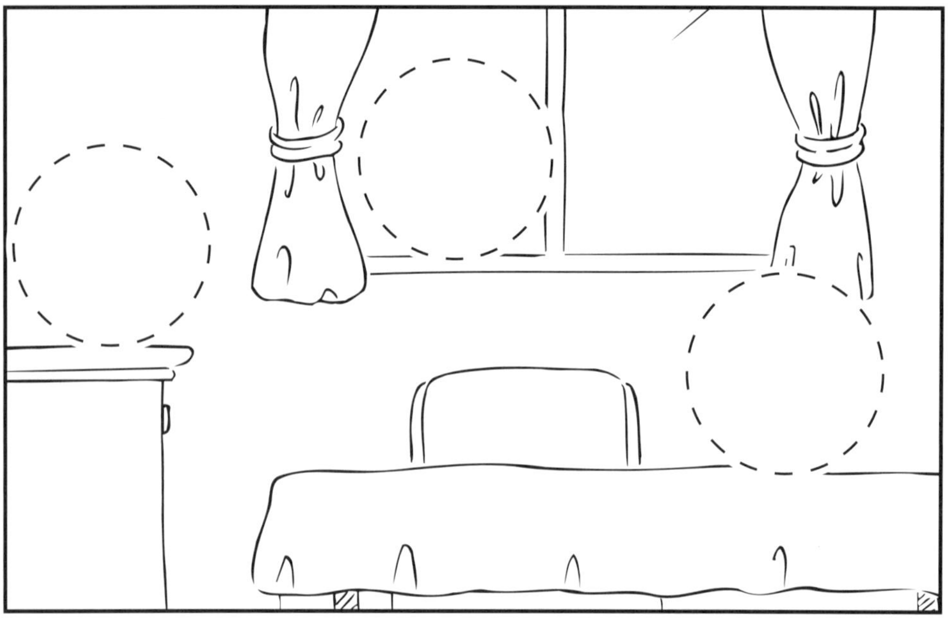

Name: Date:

Background, Middle Ground, and Foreground

Group of Seven Landscapes

Materials:

- 11 x 17" white or light-coloured paper
- construction paper of various colours
- pictures of landscapes
- scissors
- glue stick

Motivation:

To use the knowledge of background, middle ground, and foreground to create the illusion of depth in a landscape

What to Do:

1. Look through a variety of landscape prints, noticing how the foreground, middle ground, and background are different in colour, position, clarity, etc. Have the students point out objects in each of these grounds.

2. Each child should choose one landscape print. Copy the outline of the background on lighter-coloured construction paper and cut it out. This should be placed highest in the frame.

3. Look at the middle ground of the picture. Make an outline of this, cut it out, and place it halfway down the page, overlapping the background. This should be done with darker or brighter-coloured construction paper.

4. Outline and cut out the foreground and final layer of the picture on the darkest or brightest construction paper. This part should have clear, defined lines and be glued to the front, or bottom of the page, overlapping the middle and backgrounds.

Follow up:

Why do you think the background is the lightest? How does colour affect the perception of depth in a picture?

Canadian Landscape

Name: Date:

Overlapping

Objective: *To demonstrate an awareness that the overlapping of shapes is one way of creating the illusion of depth*

How do you make a flat image look three dimensional or real?

This has been the question for centuries! Thousands of years ago, the Egyptians wanted to make things look three dimensional, like today's photos. However, their attempts to create depth made their images look more like caricatures than real people.

An Egyptian Queen

Today, we know some simple techniques that help us show depth. One of them is overlapping. Put very simply, overlapping is creating the look of depth by having one shape cover a portion of another. The result gives the illusion that something is "in front of something else".

The dog covers part of the girl's body, creating depth.

By having a tree cover the corner of a house, for example, an artist can instantly make a scene look very real. This technique of overlapping is very easily done, and can bevery inspiring for young artists!

Name: Date:

Overlapping

Colour the pictures that use overlapping to create the illusion of depth.

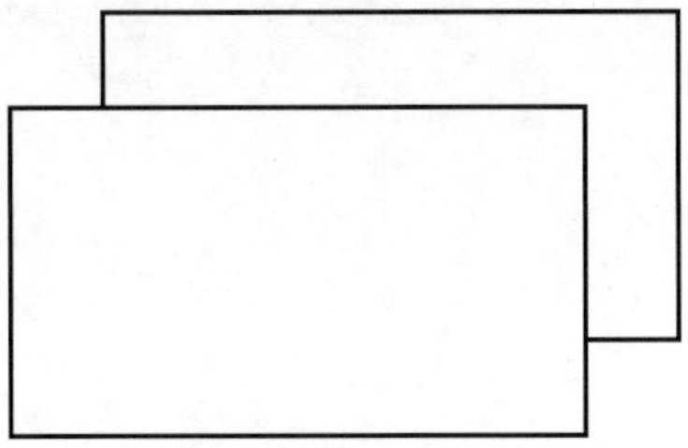
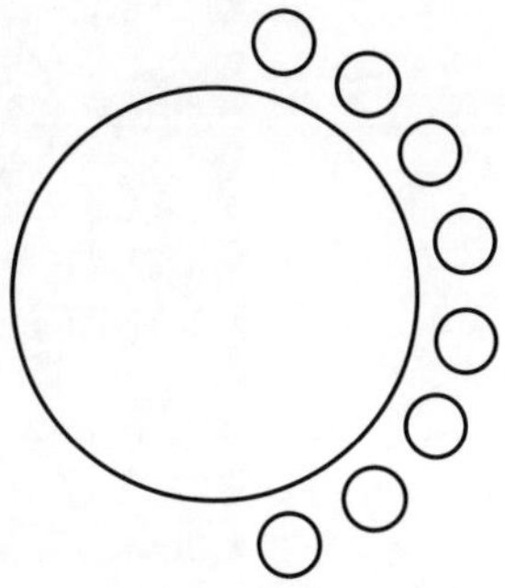
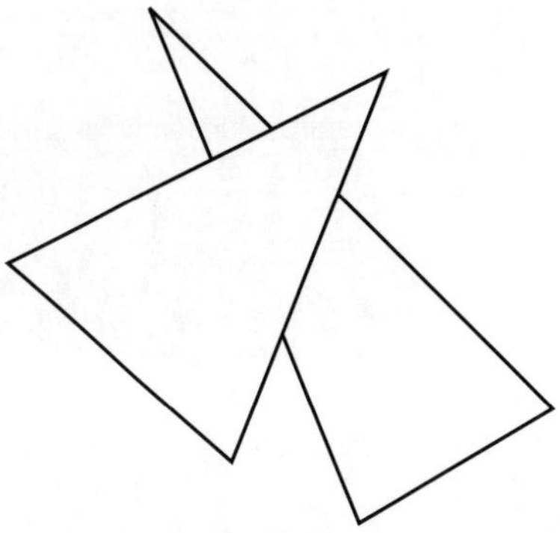

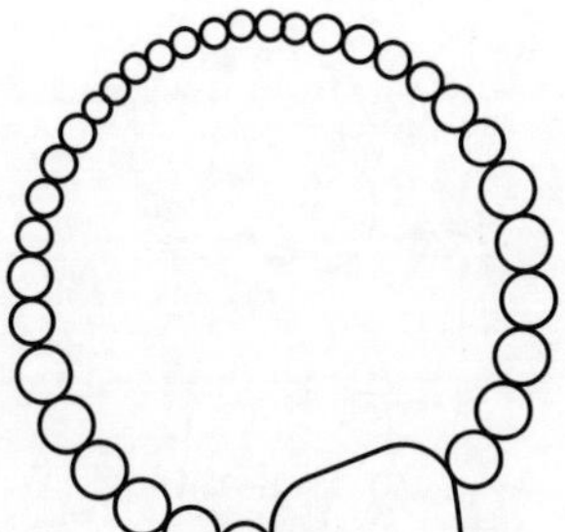
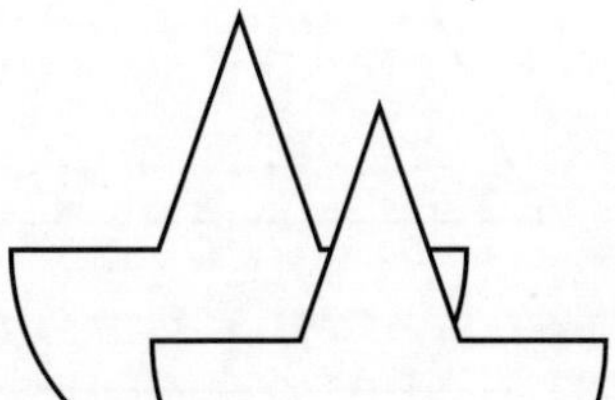

Name: Date:

Overlapping

Colour the shapes at the bottom of the page and cut them out. Then glue them in the spaces provided to make the pictures appear more realistic.

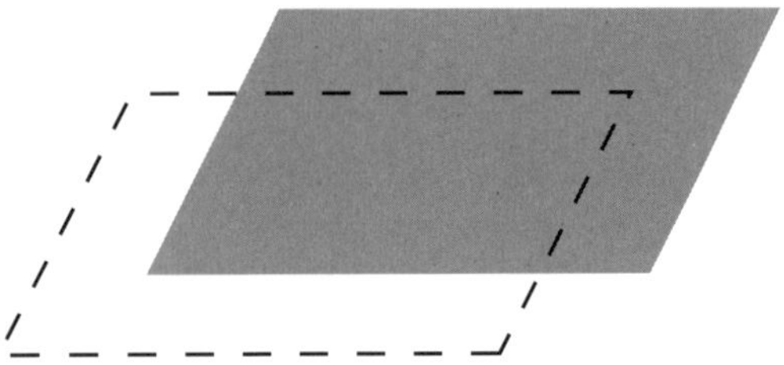
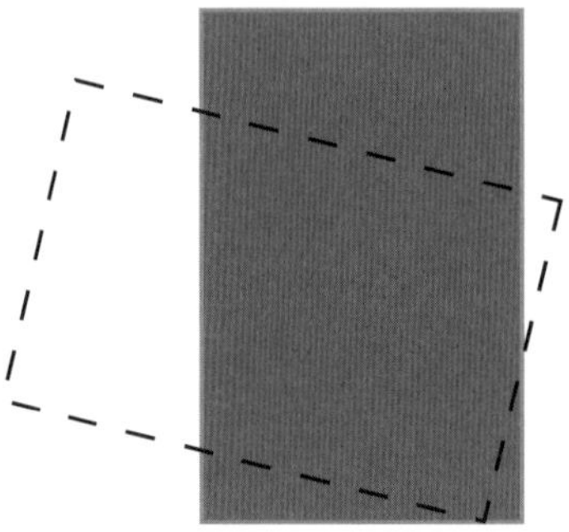
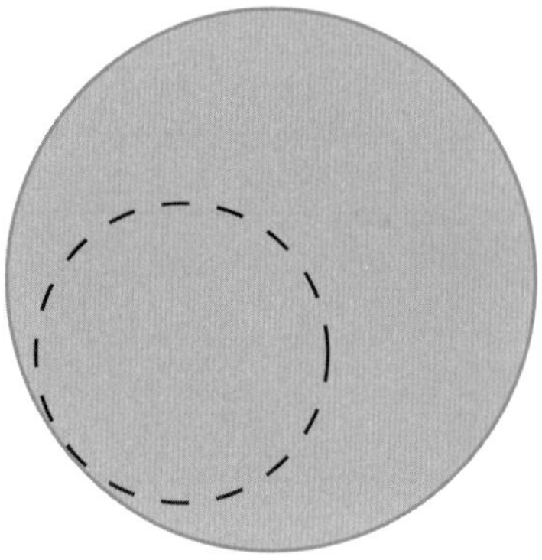

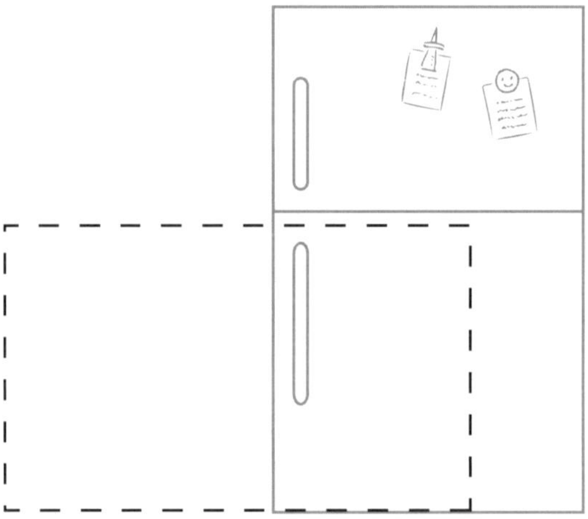

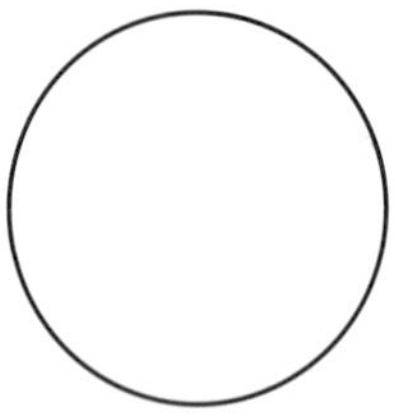
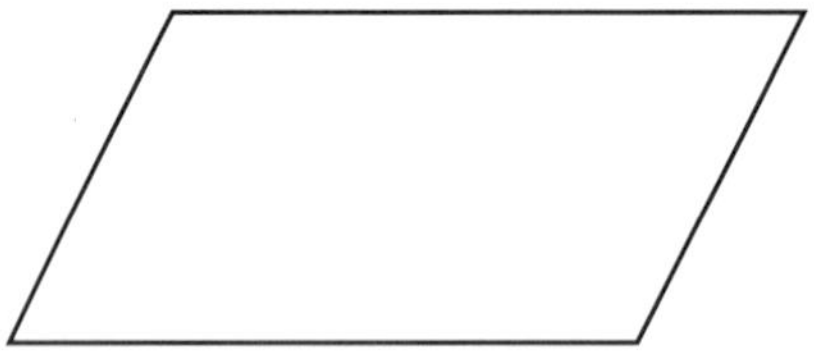

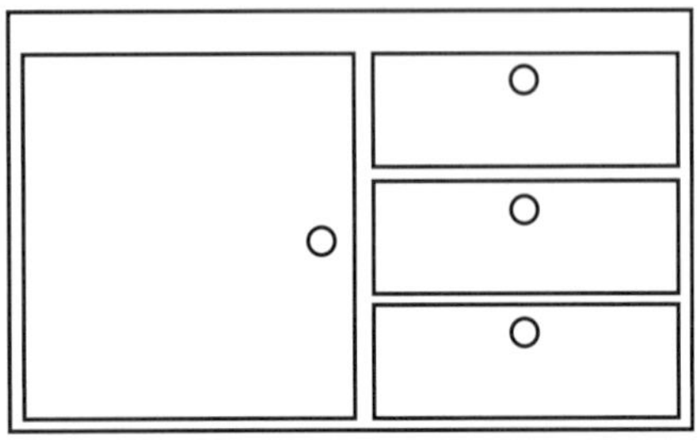

Name: Date:

Overlapping

Farmer's Harvest

Materials:

- large black construction paper
- large brown construction paper – cut in half horizontally
- 8 x 10" construction paper – various colours
- scissors
- glue
- markers
- real vegetables (or pictures of vegetables)

Motivation:

To use overlapping to make images look three-dimensional

What to Do:

1. Glue the brown construction paper to the bottom half of the black piece, creating the ground or a table.
2. Have the students outline and cut out shapes of various vegetables in different coloured construction paper. Use green for stems or leaves.
3. When gluing the pieces together, begin with the vegetable shapes that you want to be farther away. These should be closer to the top of the black construction paper.
4. Add more vegetables closer to the middle and bottom, overlapping some to show they are in front of the others.
5. The closest vegetables should overlap the others and be placed nearest the bottom of the paper.

Follow up:

Which vegetables look like they are in front or behind? How can artists use this technique to show depth in a landscape?

Name: Date:

Symmetry

Objective: *To identify symmetrical shapes in both the human-made environment and the natural world*

If you took pictures of all the students in your class, cut them straight down the middle, and mixed them up, would you be able to match them? You probably would because both sides of our faces match; they are symmetrical.

Symmetry is a type of balance in which parts or elements of an object are equal in size, shape, or other attributes. In other words, both sides look the same. Artists use symmetry because people like it when patterns are repeated and a piece looks balanced and uniform. Scientists have observed that even bumblebees prefer flowers with symmetrical petals!

Symmetry is an important part of our lives. In our houses, we appreciate the symmetry of floor tiles, chairs, and window panes. In our cities, the sides of a building mirror its front. If the women's restroom is on one side of a hallway, the men's is probably on the other side.

Sumerian art

This sense of balance is also valued in the natural world. Our bodies are symmetrical – five fingers on each hand, two eyes, ears, feet and so on. Butterflies, snowflakes, and flowers also display symmetry.

All cultures have different preference for particular patterns of symmetry. Even the earliest Sumerians were very familiar with this concept, as seen here.

Name: Date:

Symmetry

Cut out the half faces at the bottom of the page and glue them to their matching, symmetrical halves.

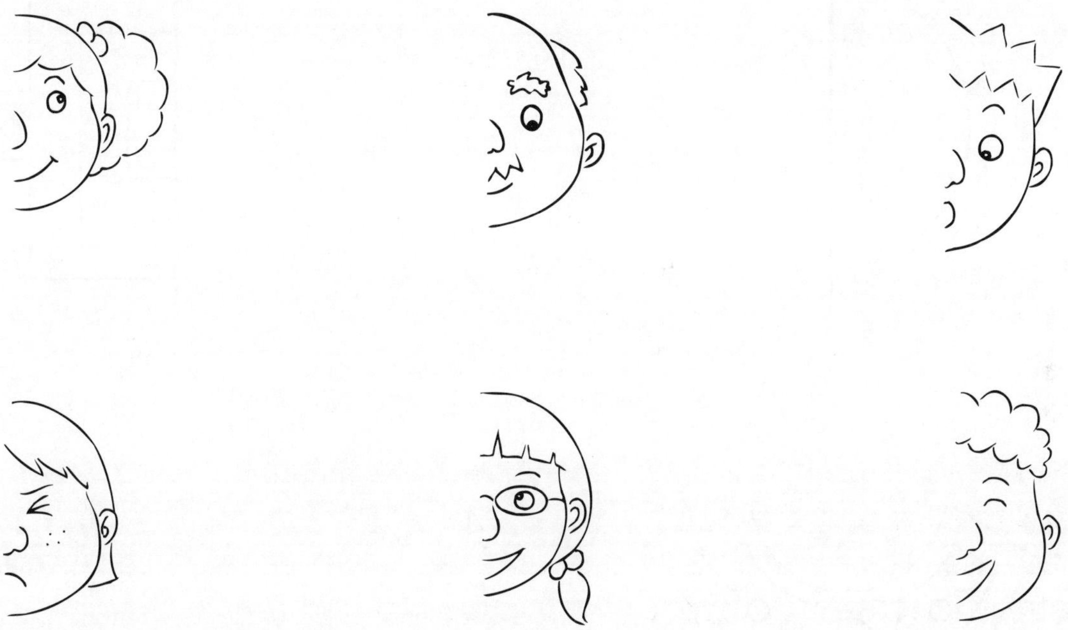

Name: Date:

Symmetry

Complete the other side of the drawing to make a symmetrical image.

1\.

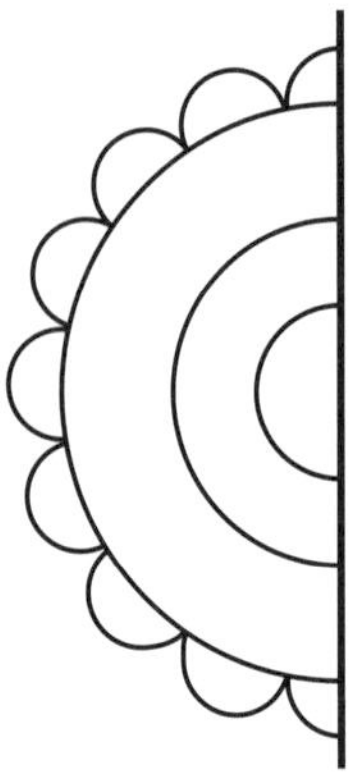

2\.

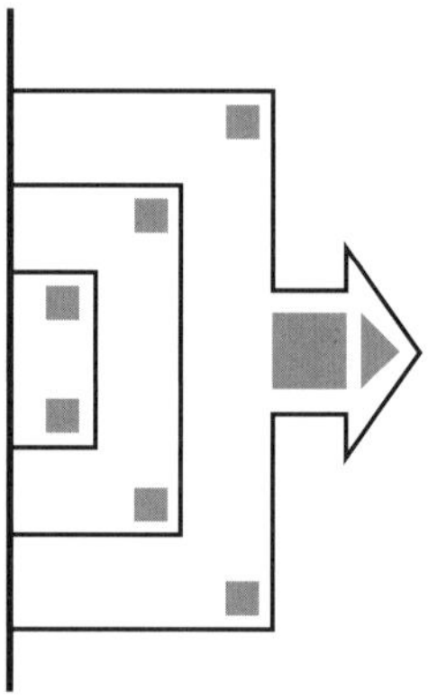

3\.

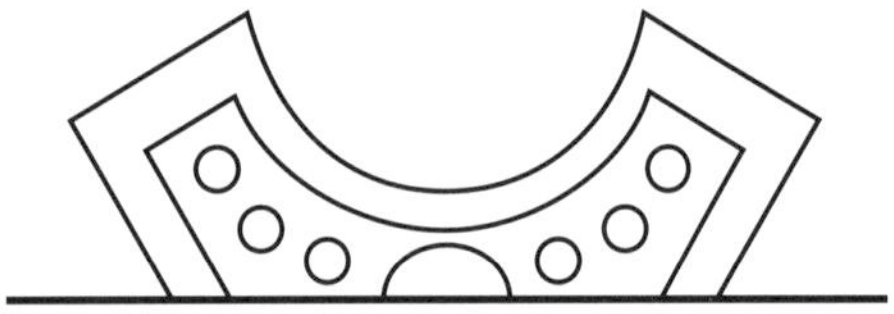

4\.

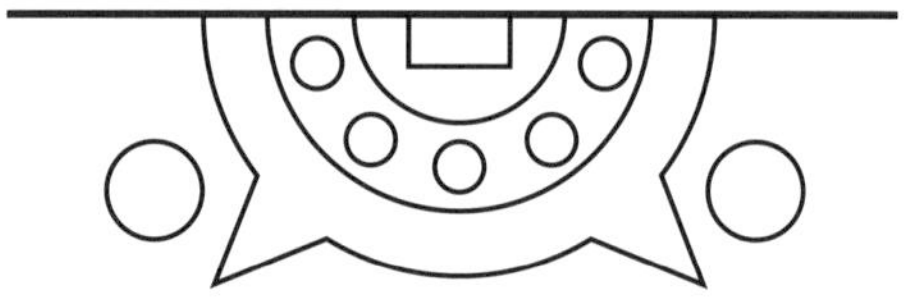

5\.

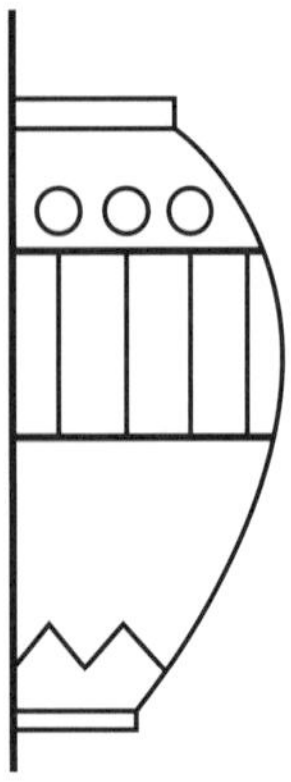

6\.

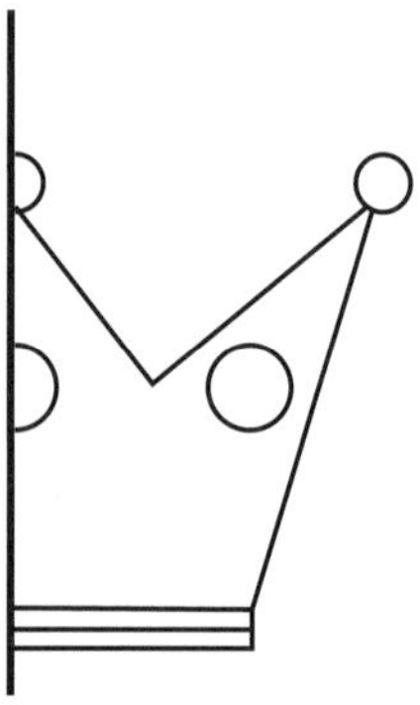

Name: Date:

Symmetry

Crazy Caribou

Materials:

- clipboard with paper and pencil
- 8.5 x 14" white paper
- various colours of tempera paint
- tray
- water
- 8.5 x 11" brown construction paper
- glue
- scissors

Motivation:

To explore symmetry in our world, both natural and human-made, by creating a unique caribou showing symmetry

What to Do:

1 Take a walk around the school, schoolyard, or neighbourhood looking for symmetry. Have the children record human-made examples and those in nature: a blade of grass, flowers, buildings, etc. Discuss.

2 Fold the construction paper in half, down the centre. Draw an outline of half of a caribou's face. Then cut it out. Open this up for its head.

3 Fold the white paper in half.

4 Make generous lines of paints of different colours, like a rainbow, on the tray.

5 Have the children make a handprint in the tray, transferring it to one side of the folded paper (thumb near fold). Close the paper, squeezing the image together.

6 Open the folded page to see both "antlers". When this is dry, cut it out and glue it to the decorated head.

Tip:

Add a speech bubble to the caribou's mouth and display the finished product on the bulletin board.

Name: Date:

Asymmetry

Objective: *To identify asymmetrical shapes in both the human-made environment and the natural world*

Two children are on a teeter-totter, and one side is heavier. Is there balance? Yes! It is just shifted.

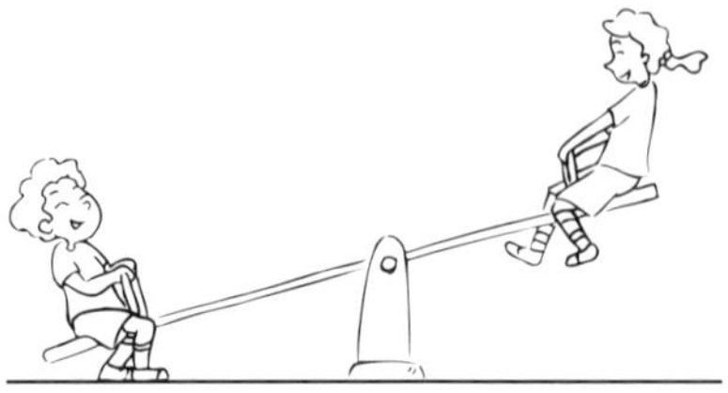

An "a" at the beginning of a word means *not* or *without*. **Asymmetry** means without symmetry – with no mirror image. It is possible to still have balance without symmetry.

When you look at a picture, what is your attention drawn to? If it wanders around somewhat evenly, there is probably balance. If you always look back to the same area, and it is not the centre of the composition, the balance of the picture may be off.

Sometimes it's easier for an artist to make the naturally pleasing lines of a symmetrical piece. But here are some tips on how you can make sure your image is asymmetrical and interesting:

- avoid putting anything of focus in the centre of the page
- be careful not to order or line things up
- avoid putting any objects exactly in corners

Asymmetry is everywhere in our world. We appreciate the old maple tree's climbing branches or the uneven stepping stones of a garden path. We also like asymmetrical variety in our house facades and skylines. Asymmetry adds interest to what we see around us.

Name: Date:

Asymmetry

A. Write whether each image is "asymmetrical" or "symmetrical" on the line provided.

1.

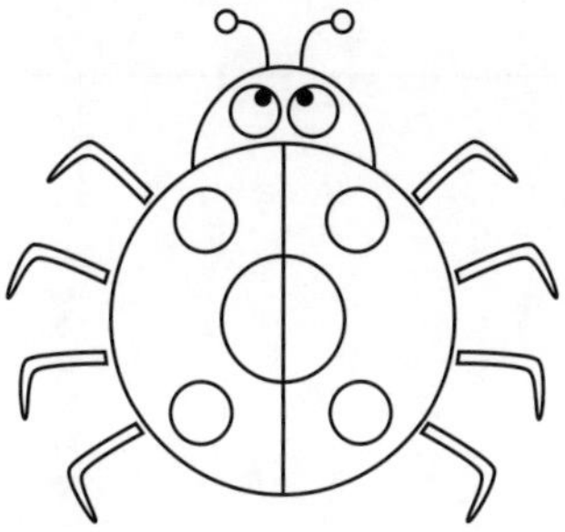

2.

3.

B. Cut out the asymmetrical hairstyles and glue them to the characters' heads.

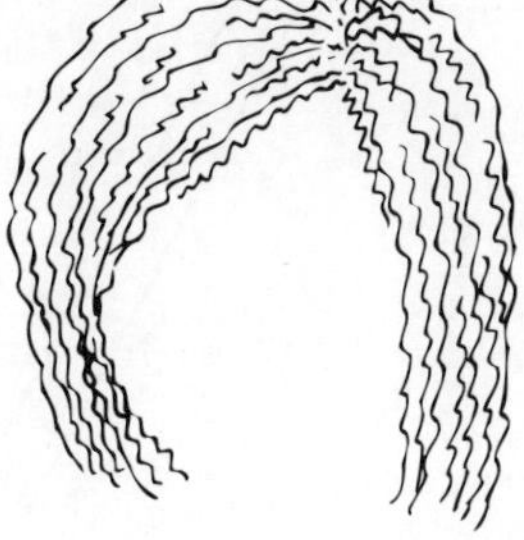

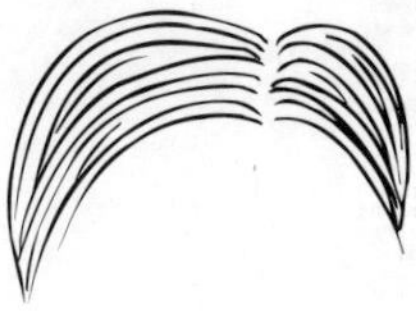

Name: Date:

Asymmetry

Add objects to this symmetrical house to make it asymmetrical.

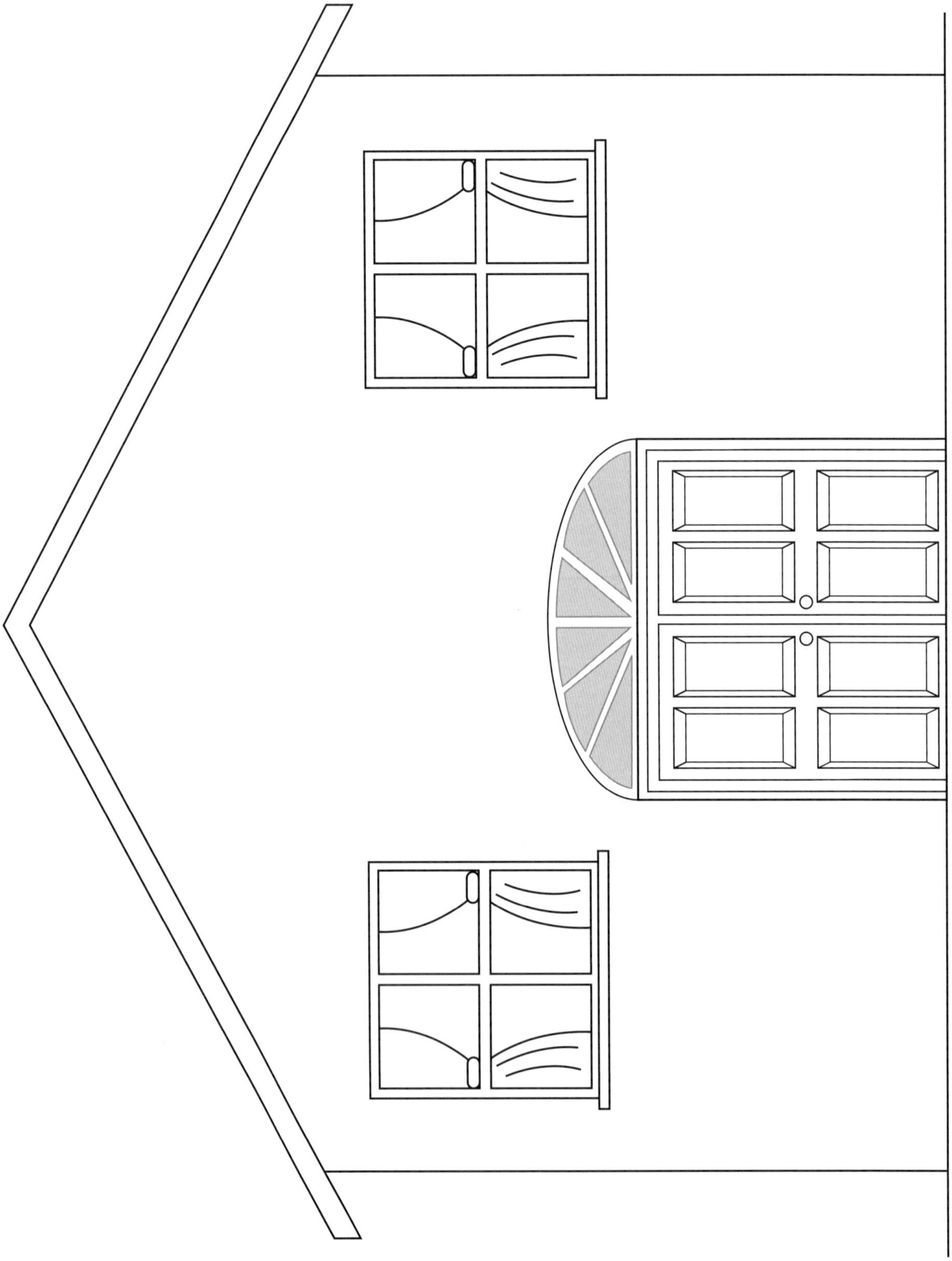

Name: Date:

Asymmetry

Roller Shapes

Materials:

- 8.5 x 11" paper
- cardboard tubes, such as toilet paper rolls (1 per student)
- foam sheets, various colours
- glue
- various colours of tempera paint
- paintbrush
- water

Motivation:

To make an asymmetrical print using rolls with various shapes

What to Do:

1 Have the students cut out a variety of small foam shapes and glue them onto the tube. Ensure that the shapes are not lined up or in a pattern.

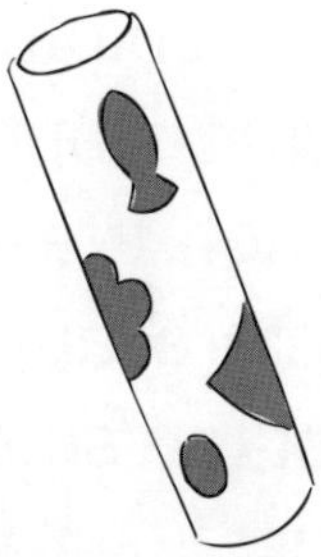

2 Paint each of the shapes different colours, and then roll the tube across the paper to see the print.

3 Repeat several times with different colours, making sure the page is filled. Encourage overlapping by rolling the tube diagonally.

Variation:

Use white glue-coated string to make a curvy, unique design on the roll. Once dry, roll the tube in a tray of paint and make a print with several different colours.

Follow Up:

How are these pictures asymmetrical? Do they seem balanced? If some look unbalanced, why do you think so?

Name: Date:

Relief Sculptures

Objective: *To distinguish between relief and free-standing sculptures (part 1)*

You may have a relief sculpture in your pocket right now! It could be one of a caribou, a beaver, or a schooner. You guessed it! Our coins have beautifully crafted relief sculptures on each of their faces. Close your eyes and feel their surfaces!

The word "relief" comes from the Italian word *relievare*, "to raise". A relief sculpture is not a type of sculpture that is free standing, but is a form that stands out from a background. It is as though these sculptures are jumping out of the picture, and you can feel their raised forms against the smooth backgrounds.

There is another type of relief sculpture known as *sunken-relief*. In this type of relief sculpture, the forms do not rise, but sink into the flat backgrounds. Next time you walk in wet sand with your bare feet or in the mud with your boots, look to see if you've made a sunken-relief sculpture.

Mount Rushmore – a famous relief sculpture

Relief sculptures can be found throughout the world. They are carved on important buildings and monuments. The ancient Greeks, Romans, and Persians are some of the people who produced beautiful relief sculptures. Mount Rushmore, the famous sculpture of four U.S. presidents in South Dakota, is a relief sculpture. In downtown Toronto, relief sculptures adorn the walls of the Bank of Nova Scotia and the Canada Post Box at the Royal York Hotel.

Name: Date:

Relief Sculptures

Circle the objects that could be considered relief sculptures.

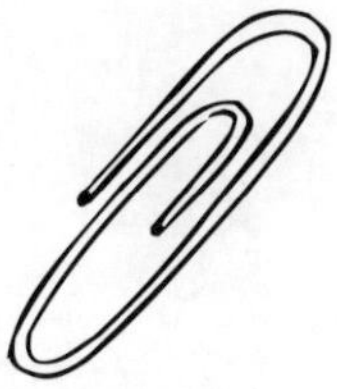

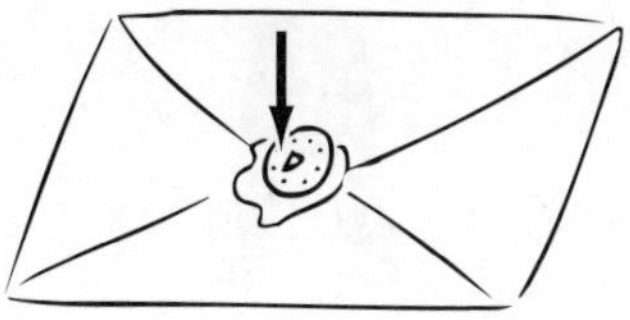

Name: Date:

Relief Sculptures

Look at the rubber stamps. Colour the stamps with sunken (lowered) forms dark colours and the ones with raised forms light colours. Then circle the correct imprint made by each stamp.

1. 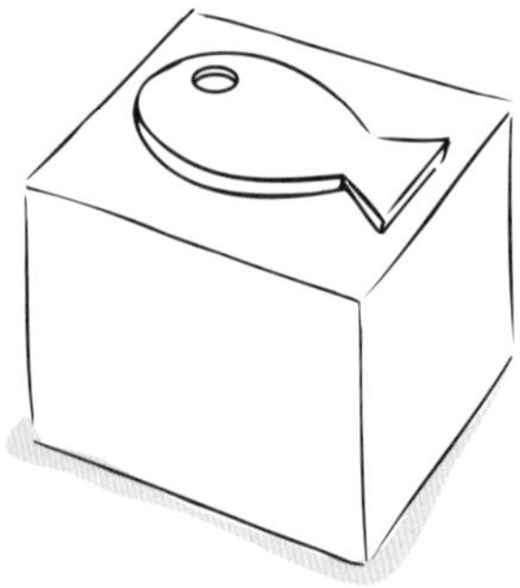 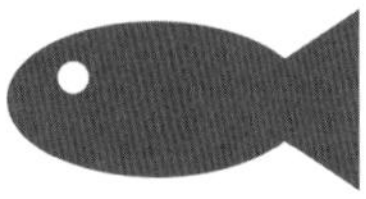 

2.   

3.   

4.   

Name: Date:

Relief Sculptures

Materials:

- popsicle stick
- plaster of Paris
- water (warm)
- large bowl
- aluminum pie plate
- large paper clip
- paint
- paintbrush

Motivation:

To make a sunken-relief sculpture of a handprint with plaster

What to Do:

1. Use the popsicle stick to mix the plaster of Paris and water in the bowl until the mixture's consistency is creamy.
2. Pour the plaster mixture into the aluminum plate (about 1" deep).
3. Have the child quickly put his or her hand onto the plaster and press down. Remove the child's hand and wash immediately.
4. At the top edge of the plaster, above the handprint, submerge the paperclip halfway into the plaster. The other half should emerge from the top so that the print can be hung on the wall.
5. Let dry overnight, and then decorate with paint, if desired.

Name: Date:

Free-standing Sculptures

Objective: *To distinguish between relief and free-standing sculptures (part 2)*

Did you know all of us are three-dimensional sculptors? We have all created a beautiful free-standing art form at some point. It may have been the extensive sandcastle you built on the water's edge or the snowman family you constructed across your front yard.

What do the Ottawa War Memorial, the Statue of Liberty, and Michelangelo's *Pieta* all have in common? They are all a type of art form called sculpture. Just like you, artists create these by carving out or putting together material, resulting in a three-dimensional piece of art.

We have looked at what relief sculptures are; free-standing sculptures have similar properties. You can feel their forms, but they don't jump out of a background. They stand on their own. You can often walk around them and feel their forms from the front, back, sides, and top. Artists refer to these free-standing sculptures as "in the round".

Famous artists throughout the centuries have created beautiful sculptures out of marble, bronze, rock, clay, ivory, and stone. They did this to record historical events and people, to immortalize beauty, and to tell stories.

The Statue of Liberty

Name: Date:

Free-standing Sculptures

Identify which artist is creating a three-dimensional piece of art by writing "sculpture" or "other" on the line. Then colour the picture.

1.

____

2.

____

3.

____

4.

____

5.

____

Name: Date:

Free-standing Sculptures

Choose which set of tools each artist needs to create his or her sculpture. Cut the set out and glue it in the appropriate circle.

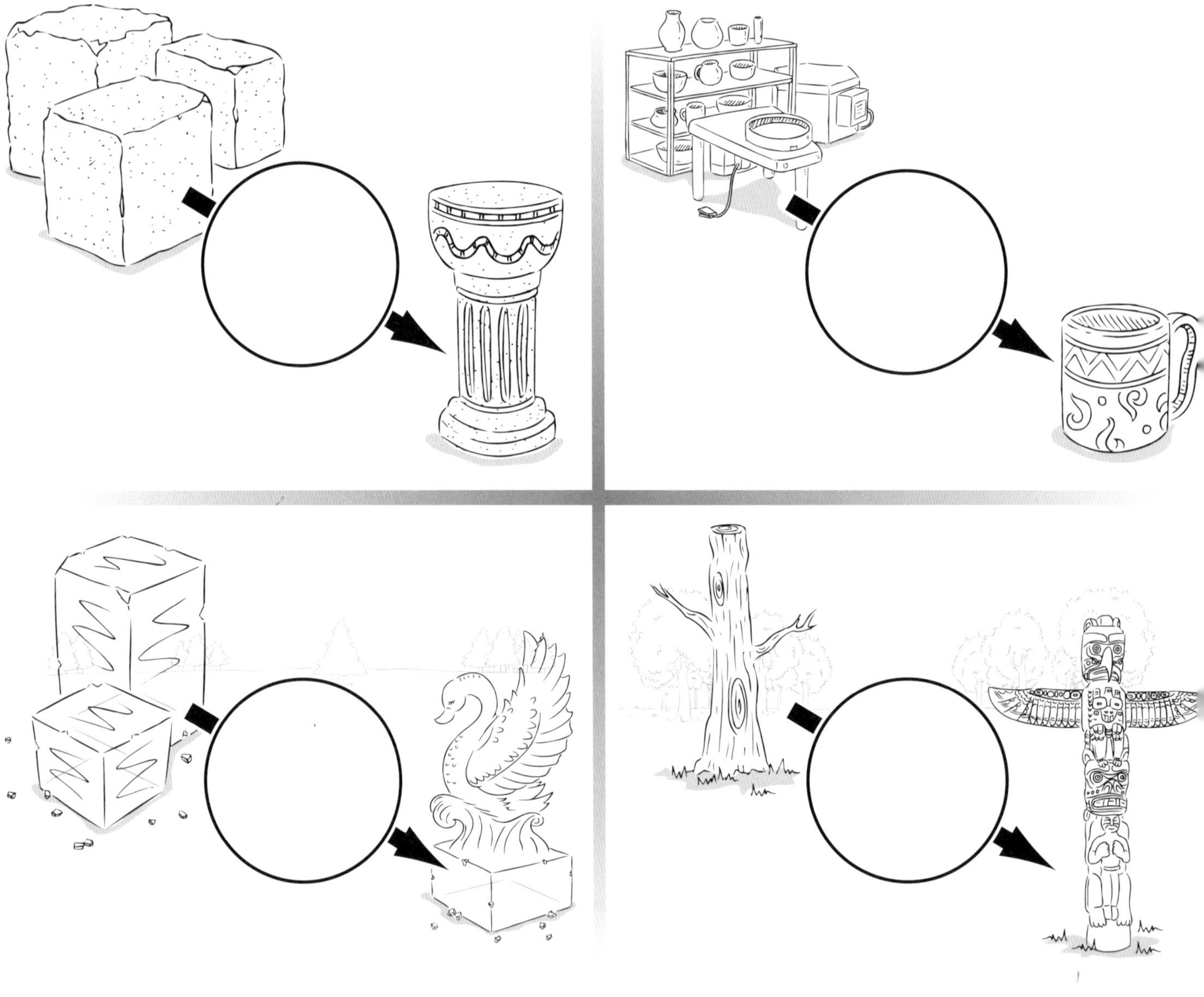

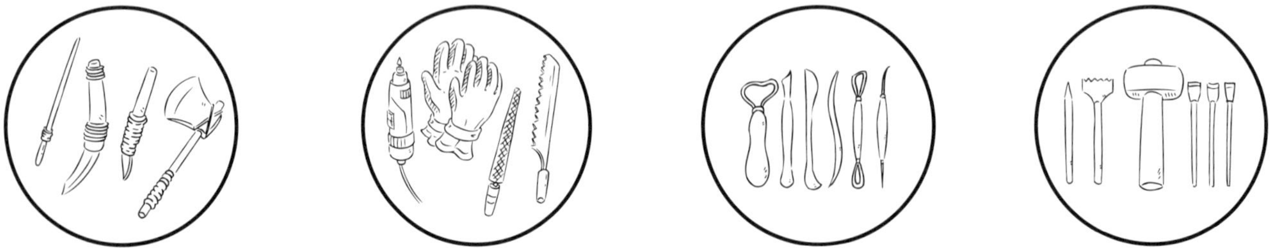

Name: Date:

Free-standing Sculptures

My Head

Materials:

- balloon
- newspaper cut into strips
- all-purpose flour
- bowl
- water (warm)
- empty margarine tub
- paint & paintbrushes

Motivation:

To make a sculpture of a head, using a variety of materials

What to Do:

1. Cover your work area with sheets of newspaper. Blow up and tie the balloon.
2. Tape the margarine tub to the bottom of the balloon to act as a stand.
3. Mix equal parts of flour and water until very smooth. Dip strips of newspaper (1″ thick) into the mixture, using two fingers to remove excess paste.
4. Cover the entire balloon and the stand, placing the strips evenly. A second layer will improve strength, if time permits.
5. Make the eyes, nose, ears, mouth, and even cheekbones and eyebrows by crumpling and moulding newspaper into forms. Use pictures, a mirror, or a fellow student to ensure correct spacing. Attach these to the balloon by smoothing pasted newspaper strips over them. Shape a pasted, crinkled sheet to look like hair and attach it to the head, if desired.
6. Allow to dry.
7. Paint the head and decorate stand (margarine tub).

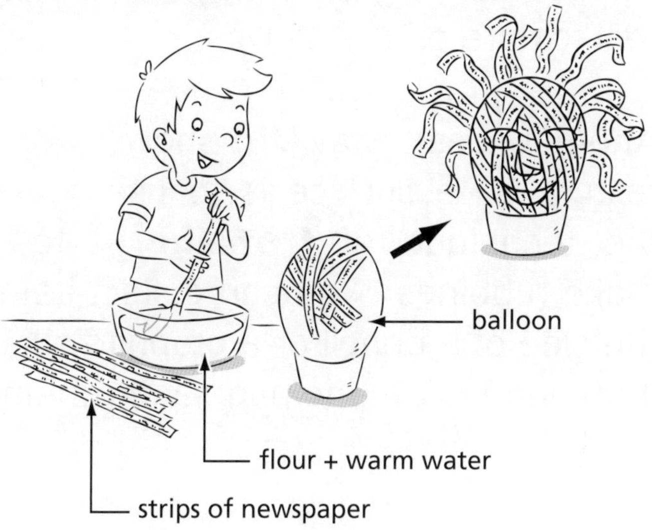

Tip:

Finish by using shiny, gold acrylic or spray paint to make it look like a bronze cast.

Name: Date:

Creating Textures

Objective: *To describe ways in which artists use a variety of tools, materials, and techniques to create texture*

How do some things give the impression of popping right off the page? Why do some art pieces seem to call out, "Touch me!"? Artistic use of texture invites the audience to interact with the work of art. There are many different tools, materials, and techniques available to artists that allow them to create this effect.

Art stores provide various materials to help create texture: gritty, sandy gels to build up canvases; charcoal to play with lighter and darker colour values; and Gesso, a plaster used as a surface preparation for painting to embed fabric in. All of these art techniques create different textures.

Some artists, such as Rembrandt, use a technique called **impasto**, which comes from the Italian word meaning "dough" or "mixture". Impasto is a thick and textured application of paint so that it is not smooth, but rough, creating very real texture on the canvas.

Another easy way to show texture on a surface is to use the technique of **frottage** – to make rubbings. You can collect items that have a unique surface and use the side of a pencil or a graphite stick to reveal their texture by placing the item underneath the page and rubbing the graphite over the page.

Name: Date:

Creating Textures

Cut out the materials that the artist can use to create texture. Then glue them on the shelves. Discard the remaining objects.

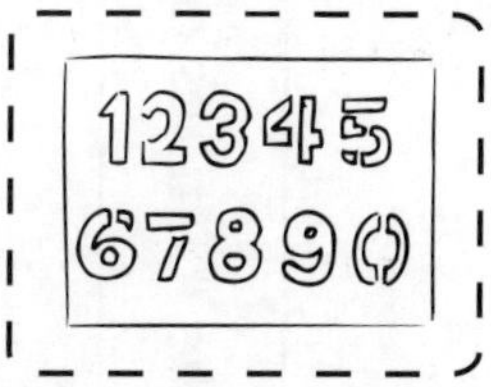

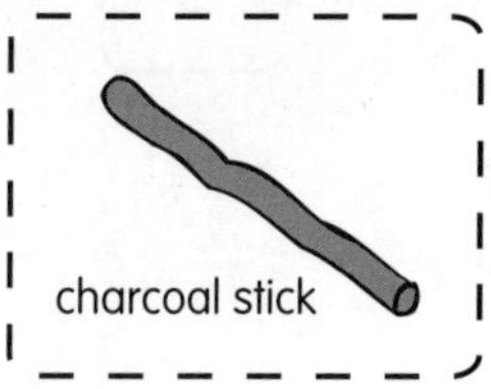

Name: Date:

Creating Textures

Apply the indicated materials to the vases.

When the mixtures have dried, feel them and compare their textures.

glue + sand

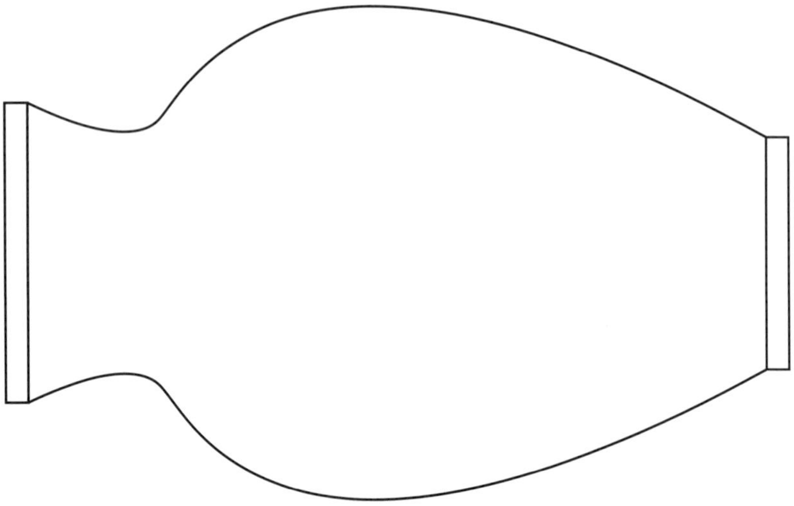

glue + tissue paper

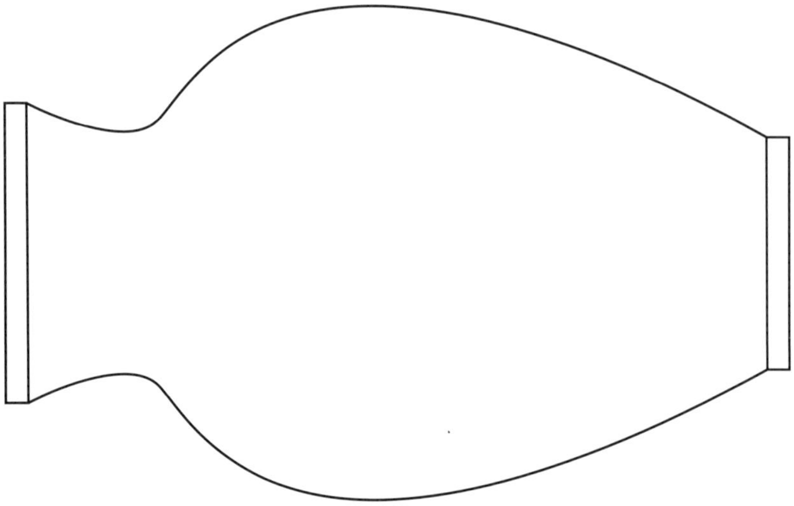

glue + oats

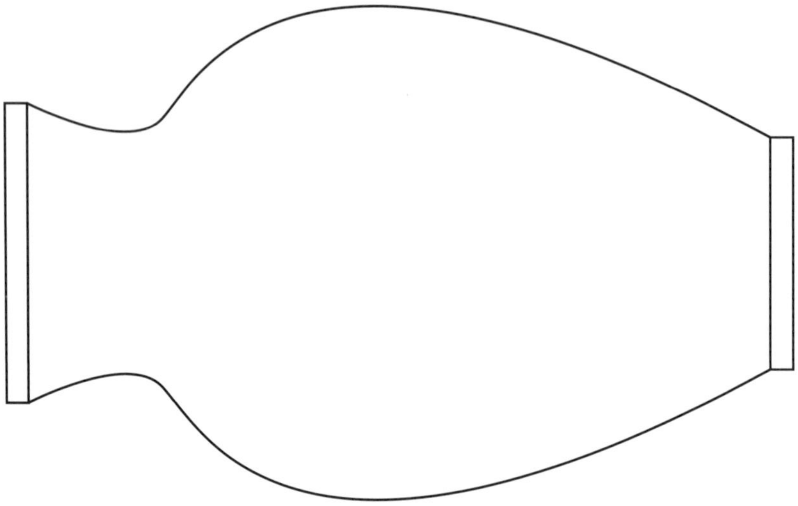

Name: Date:

Creating Textures

Impasto

Materials:

- cardboard or heavy paper (minimum 12 x 12")
- toilet paper
- white glue
- tempera or acrylic paint
- paintbrushes
- pencils
- tray

Motivation:

To use different techniques and materials to create an impasto – a thick and textured application of paint

What to Do:

1. Explain what impasto means and talk about some of the artists who have used this technique in their artwork (e.g. Rembrandt).
2. Have the students consider how they would like to design their piece, noting that a simple image will suffice (e.g. a cloud, star, or fish). Have them decide which emotion they would like to represent in their impasto (happy, sad, frightened, surprised). Draw this image on the heavy paper.
3. To prepare the "impasto", students should tear toilet paper into small pieces and mix it in a bowl with white glue.
4. Decide which parts of the image will be three dimensional and form these with the impasto (paper and glue mixture).
5. When dry, the works of art can be painted with tempera or acrylic paint. Encourage the students to use colour to bring out the emotion.
6. Spray the final work with hairspray or gloss finish.

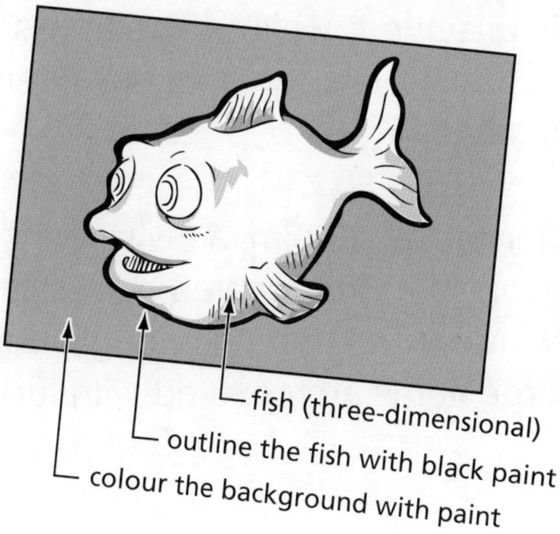

Name: Date:

Real Textures

Objective: *To describe textures that are real in art works*

If you were to describe an antique water jug to a friend, you might say, "It is white, with a handle and a large rim." Do you think you could describe it without seeing it, using another sense? What do you think of when you **look** at fur? Most likely, you want to touch it! What about sandpaper?

Real texture has a physical quality that can be *felt* as well as seen. Clay, canvas, metal, glass, and leather are unique in their textures. The bark of a tree, the grain of wood, or the surface of a pebble are all real textures in our world. We can also appreciate the sensation of human-made textures, such as cashmere sweaters, the bottom of a running shoe, or a bag of marbles.

Artists use texture to show a feeling or an idea. Roughness can feel active or unsettled, while smoothness can be restful or calming. Artists choose their materials carefully, considering what messages they want to send to their audience.

Meret Oppenheim, a Swiss artist in the 20th century, used texture to express her ideas. She created a sculpture of a cup, saucer, and spoon called *Object*. This seems common enough, but what makes this sculpture different is that all three items are covered with fur!

Name: Date:

Real Textures

A. Name two textures for each object using the given words.

smooth rough prickly sticky soft hard fuzzy wet

1. 

2. 

3. 

4. 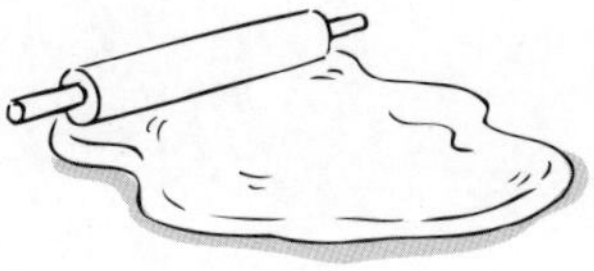

5. 

6. 

B. Name two objects usually made with each of the textured materials below.

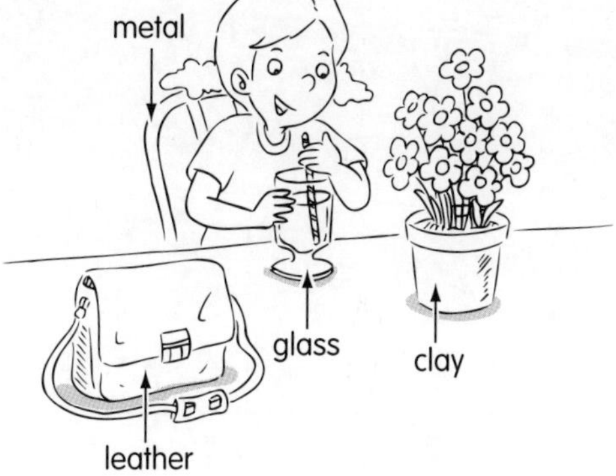

metal: ____________________

clay: ____________________

glass: ____________________

leather: ____________________

Name: Date:

Real Textures

Glue samples of the different textures indicated in the spaces provided. Then describe how each texture made you feel when you touched it. Write your answer on the line.

angry calm sad excited

a dry leaf

____

bubble wrap

____

a piece of crumpled paper

____

a cotton ball

____

Name: Date:

Real Textures

Medieval Castle Collage

Materials:

- cardboard
- cardboard cut into rectangles and squares
- wallpaper samples/thick paper
- pictures of castles
- old pencils
- silver acrylic paint
- white glue
- glue gun (assistance required)
- large piece of tree bark

Motivation:

To make a collage using a variety of materials and textures

What to Do:

1 Cover the cardboard with wall paper or other thick paper. This will be the sky or background.

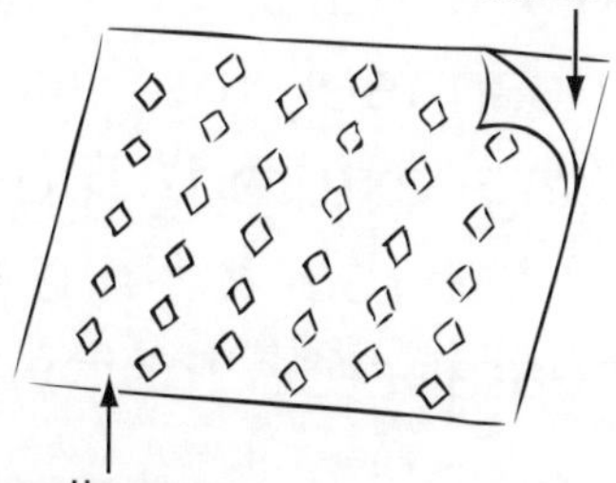

2 Look at the pictures and have the students decide how they would like to design their castle. There should be a background (e.g. tower), middle ground (e.g. wall), and foreground (e.g. gatehouse). The pencils can act as turrets.

3 Cut another piece of cardboard into rectangles, cutting along the top edges to make crenellations.

4 Have students assemble the castle, adjusting the cardboard and pencils to get their desired look. Fashion the tree bark into a hill on which the castle will sit and set it aside. Glue on the castle pieces, starting with the piece farthest back. Overlap.

5 Paint the entire castle with silver acrylic, avoiding the background.

6 Use the hot glue gun to glue on the tree bark over the bottom of the castle at the bottom of the picture. Once dry, add a detailed drawbridge or portcullis with a brown or black marker.

Name: Date:

Illusory Textures

Objective: *To describe textures that are illusory in art works (the rough texture of bark in a two-dimensional painting)*

We love textures! We want to touch, hold, and rub them. It might be hard to imagine pictures being as interesting as real textures, but they can be!

Artists use repeating dots, lines, and a variety of shapes and colours to create the **look** of texture. Visual texture, or illusory texture, is not something you can feel; the flat surface has only the effect of *looking* textured. The artists presume that you know what the real texture feels like, so they recreate its appearance in their work.

Sunflowers
Vincent Van Gogh, 1889

Vincent Van Gogh's famous *Sunflowers* is a great example of how a flat image can become three dimensional and textured with the use of different lines and colours.

To create illusory texture, a young artist must achieve a good understanding of real texture by observing its detail and surface qualities. Bring a variety of textures to the classroom to experiment with – heavy cloth, sandpaper (varied grids), fur, sponge, mesh, coins, leaves, bark, carpet samples, pinecones, and wood (grain and bark). Use the side of a crayon (paper removed) to create rubbings. Make a "What Texture Am I?" book, with one rubbing per page, and switch with another student.

Name: Date:

Illusory Textures

Use the illusory textures provided to decorate the picture below.

Name: Date:

Illusory Textures

Using the materials indicated, colour all the leaves with the same colour – either green, yellow, or brown. Then answer the question.

pastel

marker

pencil crayon

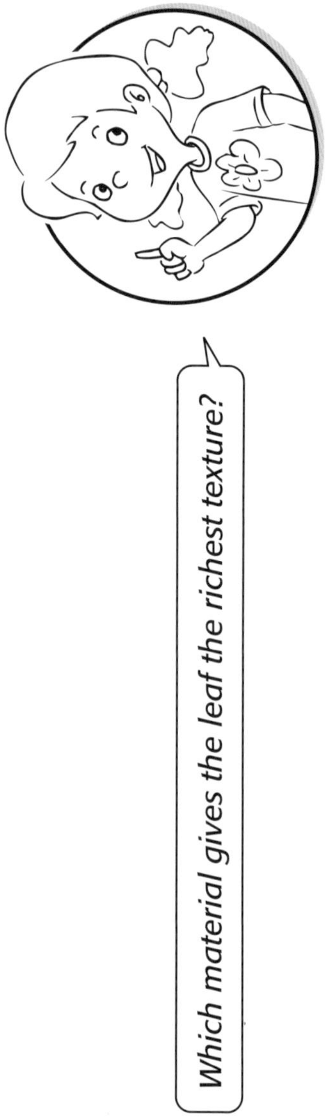

Name: Date:

Illusory Textures

Flowers in a Vase

Materials:

- paper
- sponges with large holes
- leaves, either real or fabric
- thin, 6 – 8″ branches or sticks
- tempera paint
- trays (various sizes)
- water

Motivation:

To create a two-dimensional image of a vase of flowers, using different techniques to create textures

What to Do:

1 Have the students draw the outline of a vase near the bottom of the page, with one colour of paint. Gradually add small amounts of white to the painted outline, and blend the colour inwards, making lighter tints.

2 Encourage the students to plan out their composition, deciding the colours of the flowers, ways in which the branches will reach out of the vase, etc.

3 Create a station where the students can dip the branches in paint, making a print of the stems in the vase.

4 Dip the leaves in the paint, and make prints of the leaves along the stems. Use the sponges to create textured flowers of various colours on the branches. Add more leaves around the flowers to finish the look of a freshly picked bouquet.

painting the vase

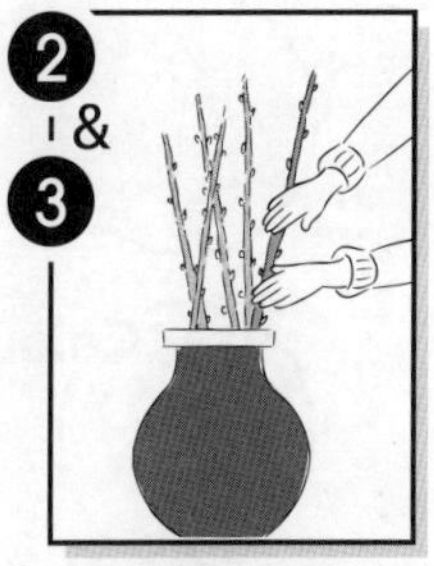

making prints of the stems

using sponges to create textured flowers and leaves to make prints

Tip:

Flowers in a Turquoise-Coloured Vase c.1905 by Odilon Redon is a great reference for this activity.

Follow up:

What effects do these materials and techniques (printing, sponging, blending) create?

Name: Date:

Elements of Design

Objective: *To identify elements of design in a variety of natural and human-made objects*

The elements of design are all around us. Looking outside, we see the form of a tree, the colour and value of its leaves, the texture of its bark, and the space that surrounds it. These are all part of what makes it real and magnificent. We can also observe these elements in human-made objects: the forms of our skyscrapers, their smooth textured walls, the space that surrounds them, and the hues reflected in their metal and glass. Artists re-create these in different ways to make their work stand out from the rest.

The elements of design:

Line
the visual line left by a moving point

Form
a sculptural or three-dimensional shape

Colour
the particular hue that is seen when light is reflected off an object

Value
the lightness or darkness of a colour

Texture
the actual feel or the illusion of a feeling of an object or a material

Space
the area around, within, or between images or elements

Name: Date:

Elements of Design

A. Name three elements of design.

______________________ ______________________ ______________________

B. Find a picture from an old magazine. Cut it out and glue it in the box below. Then write down the elements of design you see in the picture in the space provided.

Elements of Design

Name: Date:

Elements of Design

Answer the questions below.

1. What do the lines make?

a. 

____

b. 

____

2. What forms are these?

a. 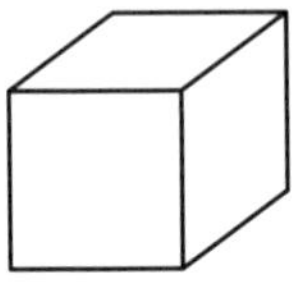

____

b. 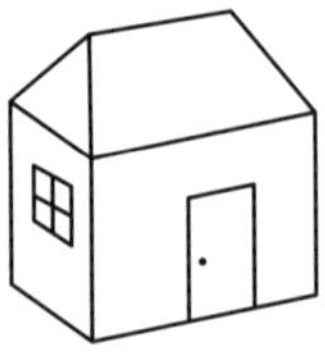

____

3. What colours would these be?

a. 

____

b. 

____

4. What texture would these have?

a. 

____

b. 

____

Name: Date:

Elements of Design

My Dream Vacation

Materials:

- 18 x 18″ scrapbook page
- construction paper in various colours
- tissue paper in various colours
- travel magazines or brochures
- black, fine-tipped markers
- collage materials (scraps of fabric, yarn, ribbon, corrugated cardboard, etc.)
- scissors
- white glue

Motivation:

To use as many elements of design as possible to showcase an environment (natural or human-made)

What to Do:

1 Discuss the idea of a dream vacation. Give the students time to decide where they would most like to go if there was no limitation on distance, time, or money.

2 Encourage the students to plan out a picture brochure or scrapbook page of this destination. As the objective is to use each element of design to make the page attractive, ask the following questions:

What will be the subject (natural or human-made) of each image? Which element of design will be the focus for each? What materials will be used?

3 Encourage the students to use a large variety of the materials available to make their collage.

4 Use markers to label the different images, and add a title.

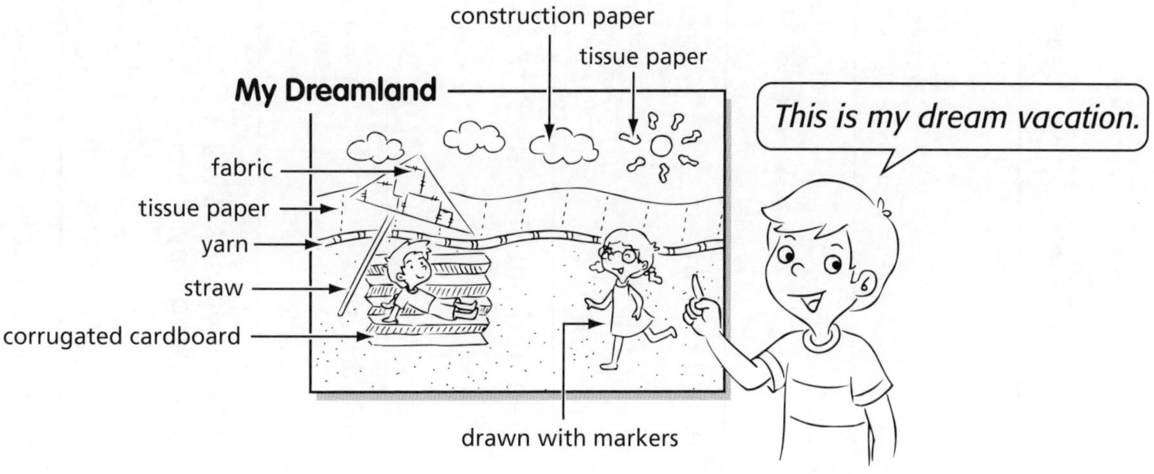

Name: Date:

Evaluating Tools and Materials

Objective: *To study the strengths and limitations of different art tools and materials, demonstrate their proper use, and see how they can create effects*

Tools/Materials	Uses	Strengths	Weaknesses
Pencil	Shading and blending (side), drawing preliminary sketches, cross-hatching and point drawing, outlining (tip)	Universal, inexpensive, shades blend easily, can be erased	Black and white only, smudges (does not last), lead breaks easily
Charcoal	Blending, shading, surface rubbing, outlining	Greater area of coverage (on its side), tonal variety	Messy, breaks easily, only black
Pencil crayon	Making variations in tone, creating multi-line images, shading, cross-hatching, dot drawing, outlining	Colour, universal, clean, creates precise lines and various shades	Limited blending, no pure colour
Coloured felt-tip pens	Creating solid, brilliant-coloured images, blurred effects with water, outlining	Distinct lines, brilliant colours	No variation of line width or density
Paintbrushes	Blending, stippling, creating detail, creating texture, washes	Varied widths of strokes	Restricted ground surface (must be thicker/hold water)
Plasticine/self-drying modelling clay	Free form sculptures, relief, planning models	Manipulate into any form with a variety of tools, easy to add on to, variety of colours, some can be painted, can show textures, is three-dimensional	Does not last, some dye skin and work surfaces
Found materials	Sculpture, relief, rubbings, collages	Natural look, variety of combinations, unique textures	Difficult to adjust or cut, adhesive may not last

Name: Date:

Evaluating Tools and Materials

Which material would work best to create each of the following pieces of art? Choose your answer from the word bank and write it on the line.

Tools / Material

pencil charcoal pencil crayon coloured, felt-tip pens

paintbrush + paints plasticine found materials spray paint

1. a frottage ____________________

2. a mosaic ____________________

3. graffiti art ____________________

4. a picture showing heavy lines ____________________

5. a sketch of a cup on paper ____________________

6. a small, colourful picture ____________________

7. a collage ____________________

8. 

____

Name: Date:

Evaluating Tools and Materials

Colour the stars using the materials indicated. Then answer the question.

Pencil

Marker

Paintbrush

Which material works best for each size?

________________	________________	________________
the smallest star	medium-sized star	the biggest star

Name: Date:

Evaluating Tools and Materials

Plasticine Scene

Motivation:

To use plasticine and a variety of tools to create a book cover

Materials:

- large plastic lid, CD case, or sheet of heavy cardboard
- plasticine
- tools (toothpick, plastic knife, toothbrush, comb, ruler)
- paper and pencil

What to Do:

1 Encourage the students to plan out the setting of their books, whether it be a farm yard, a jungle, a city neighbourhood, etc. Emphasize the use of simple shapes and lines for their composition. Have them sketch the scene on paper first.

2 Practise handling the plasticine; squish and knead it to make it softer. Try mixing colours and adding white; reserve specific pieces to be used for the images on the cover.

3 Use the CD case or heavy cardboard as a foundation for the background. Start by taking small amounts of plasticine and spreading them out with your thumbs to create the sky and ground (background). Continue to add small pieces until the foundation is covered. Vary the tones and direction of blending (e.g. swirls) to add interest and to show emotion.

4 Use your hands to make the images in the middle ground and, lastly, the foreground. A round, flat piece can become a sun or part of a puffy cloud. Roll clay and flatten it to make branches, sun rays, or fence posts.

5 Use tools to create texture, like using a toothpick to scrape lines down the front of a barn door or using the teeth on a plastic knife to make the wind swirl. A small comb or fork can scratch a grassy or furry texture. Use toothbrush bristles to create a fuzzy look. A thick ruler edge can cut straight lines for the edges of buildings.

Name: Date:

Using Tools and Materials to Create Effects

Objective: *To use tools and materials to create effects*

There are endless materials that can be used to create amazing effects in art. Some interesting options include:

- Carving an eraser or drawing on a styrofoam tray to create printing blocks
- Drawing with white wax crayons or oil pastels, and painting over the image with watercolour to create a resist
- Creating textured paper by making surface rubbings of various materials or by dragging a toothbrush or comb across a freshly painted page
- Using a straw to blow paint across paper
- Tracing and fitting shapes together to form repeating patterns
- Using tissue paper with a glue and water mixture to cover the surface of a three-dimensional object, or overlapping tissue paper shapes to create different colour tones
- Using pastels to give a feathery look to an ink drawing
- Assembling torn paper and found materials to make an interesting, three-dimensional collage
- Applying plastic wrap to a wash of acrylic paint and allowing it to dry before removing it, revealing a speckled effect
- Cutting out paper shapes, and colouring over and beyond their outlines, leaving negative images
- Using crayons to draw patches of colour on thick paper, and painting over with black tempera; then, scratching an image on the surface to reveal the colours underneath

Name: Date:

Using Tools and Materials to Create Effects

Match the effects with the tools used to create them. Cut out the pictures and glue them in the correct boxes.

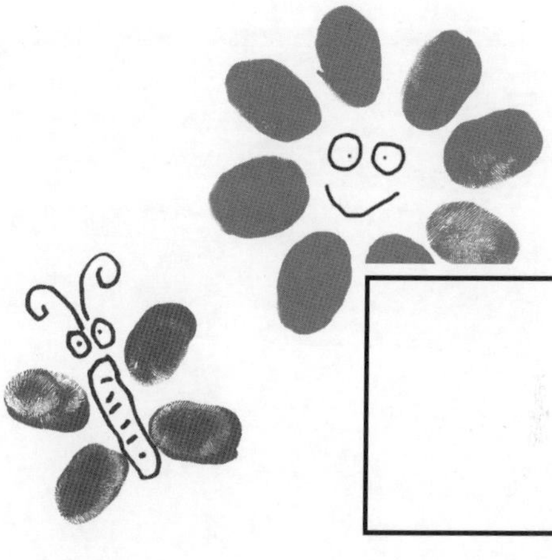

Name: Date:

Using Tools and Materials to Create Effects

For each pair of shapes, tear out one and cut out the other. Then glue them beside each other on the page. Consider the effect created by cutting paper as opposed to tearing it. Add colour to emphasize the contrast.

diamond

leaf

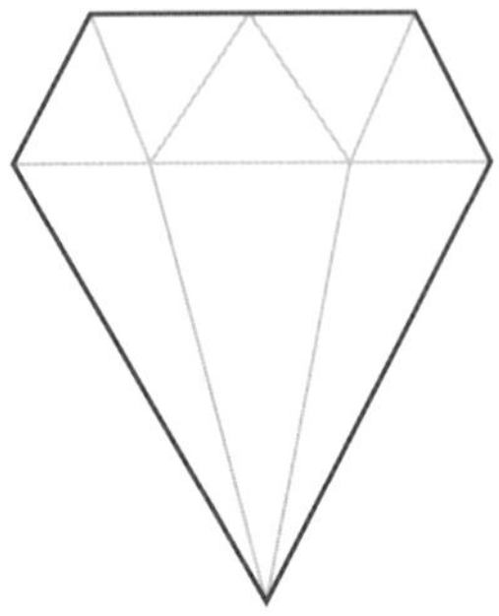

Name: Date:

Using Tools and Materials to Create Effects

Motivation:

To observe the effects of salt on watercolour paints

Materials:

- newspaper
- pencil
- drawing paper
- watercolour paint
- paintbrush
- salt

What to Do:

1. Cover your work area with newspaper.
2. Sketch a picture of your choice on the paper.
3. Paint over your drawing with the watercolour paint.
4. Sprinkle salt onto the wet watercolour paint, and let it dry.
5. When dry, observe the effects of the salt on watercolour paint.

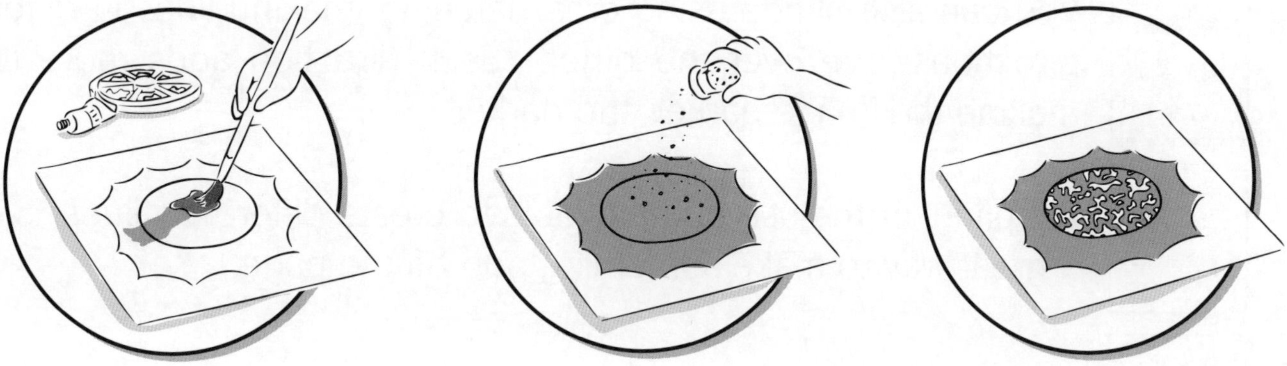

Follow up:

Discuss the scientific reasoning that explains why this effect occurs.

Name: Date:

Using Techniques to Create Effects

Objective: *To use techniques to create effects, and to demonstrate an understanding of the proper and controlled use of art tools, materials, and techniques*

You can bring life to an image by following these handy tips:

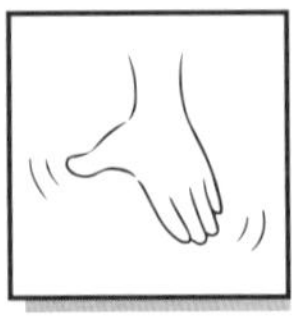

Use short, continuous lines to show movement in your drawings.

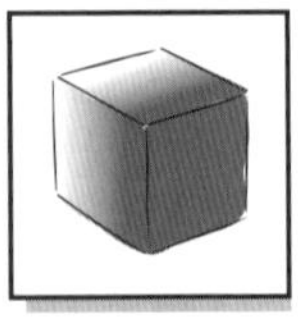

Use a pencil, a pencil crayon, or charcoal to shade or change the value of an object, making it look three dimensional. On flat surfaces, such as a cube's sides, change the values sharply from one side to the next. On a rounded surface, gradually change the value, with the lightest part facing the light source.

You can also shade using crosshatching: making lines in different directions, one over the other. Each direction adds more tone, making the image darker and darker.

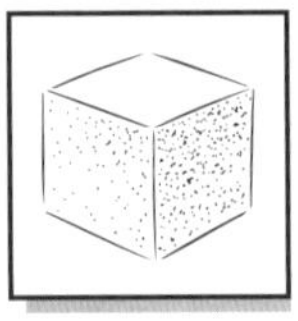

Stippling, or the use of many dots to create different values, is also a great way to make something pop off the page.

Paint with a sponge to give your work a unique look.

Flick the brush's bristles onto paper to make the paint splatter.

With heavier paints, such as oil paint, a palette knife can be used to spread the paint in ridges across the canvas.

Name: Date:

Using Techniques to Create Effects

Apply the following techniques to make the circles on the right three-dimensional spheres.

Hatching

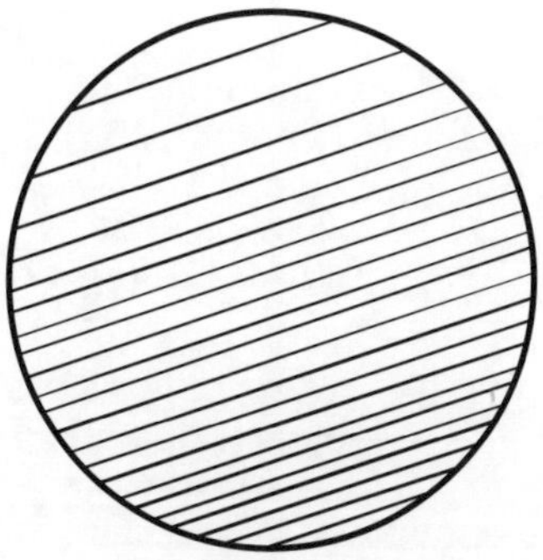

Stippling

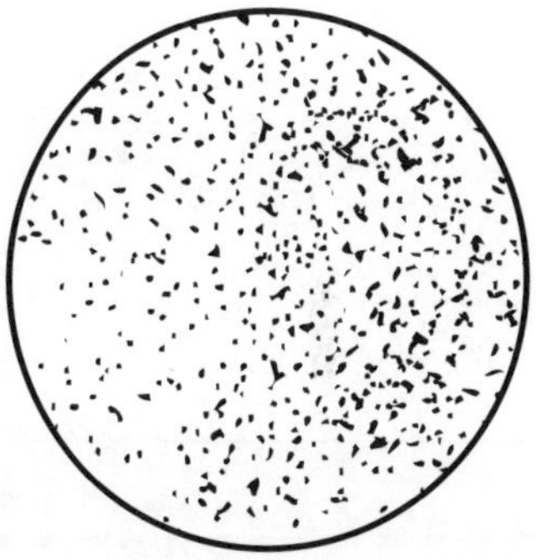

Shading

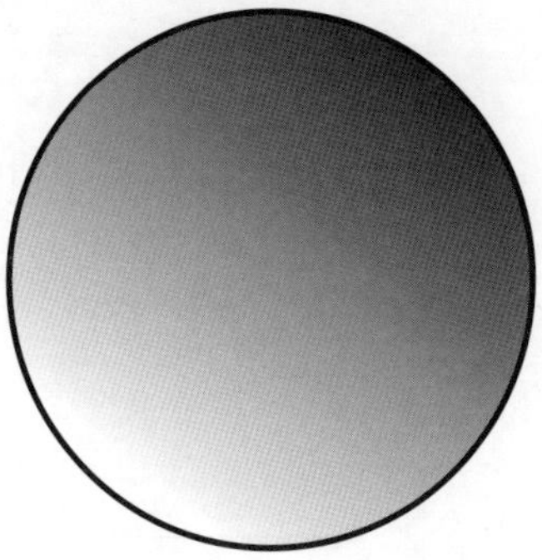

Crosshatching

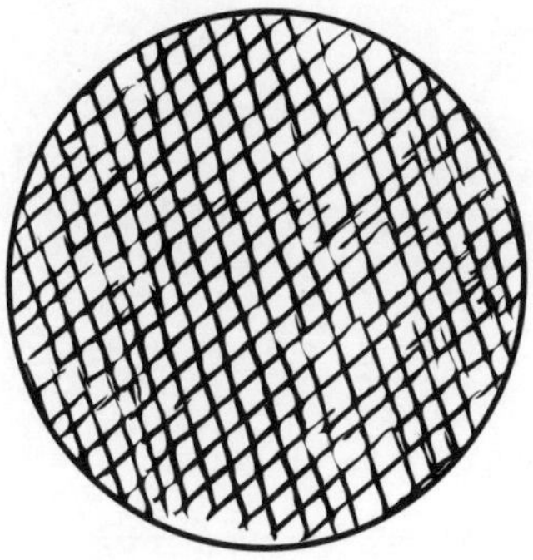

Name: Date:

Using Techniques to Create Effects

Identify the technique used to shade each picture. Write the answer on the line.

stippling   hatching   cross hatching   shading

____

____

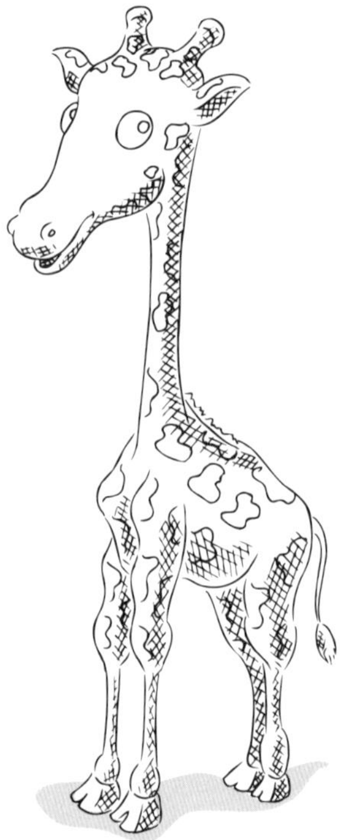

____

____

____

____

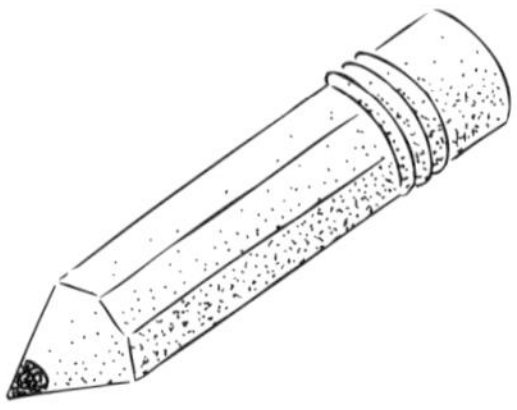

____

Name: Date:

Using Techniques to Create Effects

Create a 3-D shelf

Materials:

- 6 x 6″ white paper cut-out
- 3 x 3″ Bristol board cut-out
- pencil
- ruler
- magazines or flyers
- glue stick

Motivation:

To use shading to create the illusion of depth on a flat page

What to Do:

1 Have the students practise creating a light, medium, and dark value of grey by applying pressure on the side of the pencil.

2 Position the 3″ square in the top right corner and trace it.

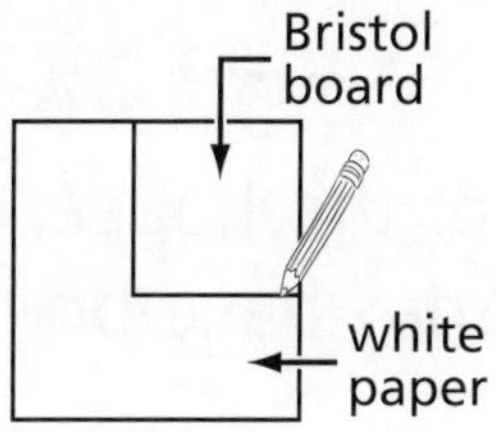

3 Draw a diagonal line connecting the bottom left corner of the 3″ square to the bottom left corner of the larger (6″) square.

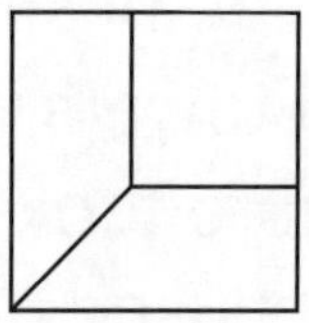

4 Shade the 3″ square with a medium value of grey. Shade the shape below this with a very dark value of grey. Shade the shape to the left with a light value of grey.

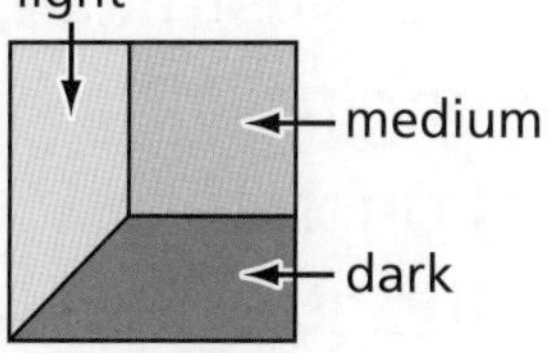

5 Cut a picture of a household item out of a magazine and glue it to the picture so that it is sitting in the darkly shaded section.

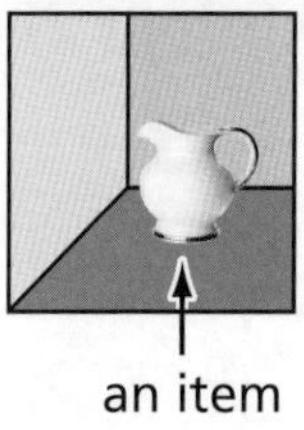

Name: Date:

Artists' Use of Elements in Architecture

Objective: *To describe how artists have used elements of design, tools, materials, and techniques in diverse styles, historical periods, and forms of media*

What if your house was made completely out of sticks, bark, and grass? Imagine spending the winter in it! Architects and builders of the past had very different tools and materials than we have today.

For example, the Ontario First Nations people used to build houses almost 80 feet long to house many families! These longhouses were supported by poles driven into the ground, and strips of bark were used for the walls. The door, usually at one end of the house, was covered by animal skins, and the roof may have been covered with bark and twigs.

This type of structure is very different from one of today's tallest towers, the CN Tower! Just the excavation of this structure took a huge team of people to complete. The project used new technology and building techniques. Its construction was considered to be incredible engineering at the time; large amounts of concrete and metal were used to make the structure stable. When the CN Tower was completed in 1975, it became the world's tallest free-standing structure.

Name: Date:

Artists' Use of Elements in Architecture

Decide which materials were used to create the following structures. Write the answers on the lines.

modelling clay and sticks **blocks** **cardboard**

wood **cards** **sand**

1. 

____

2. 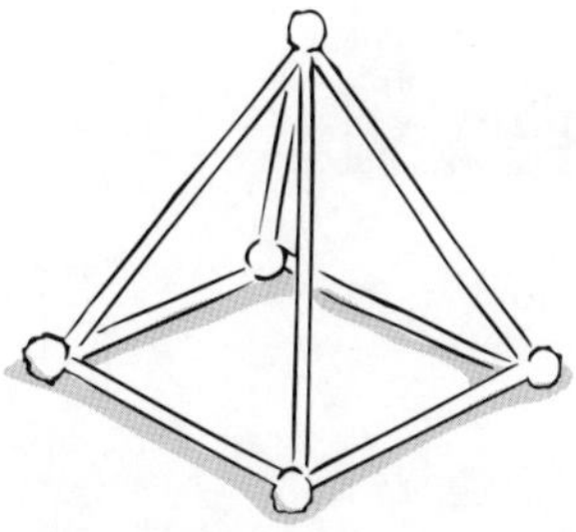

____

3. 

____

4. 

____

5. 

____

6. 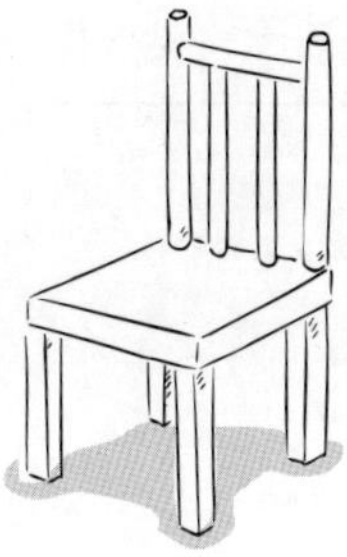

____

Name: Date:

Artists' Use of Elements in Architecture

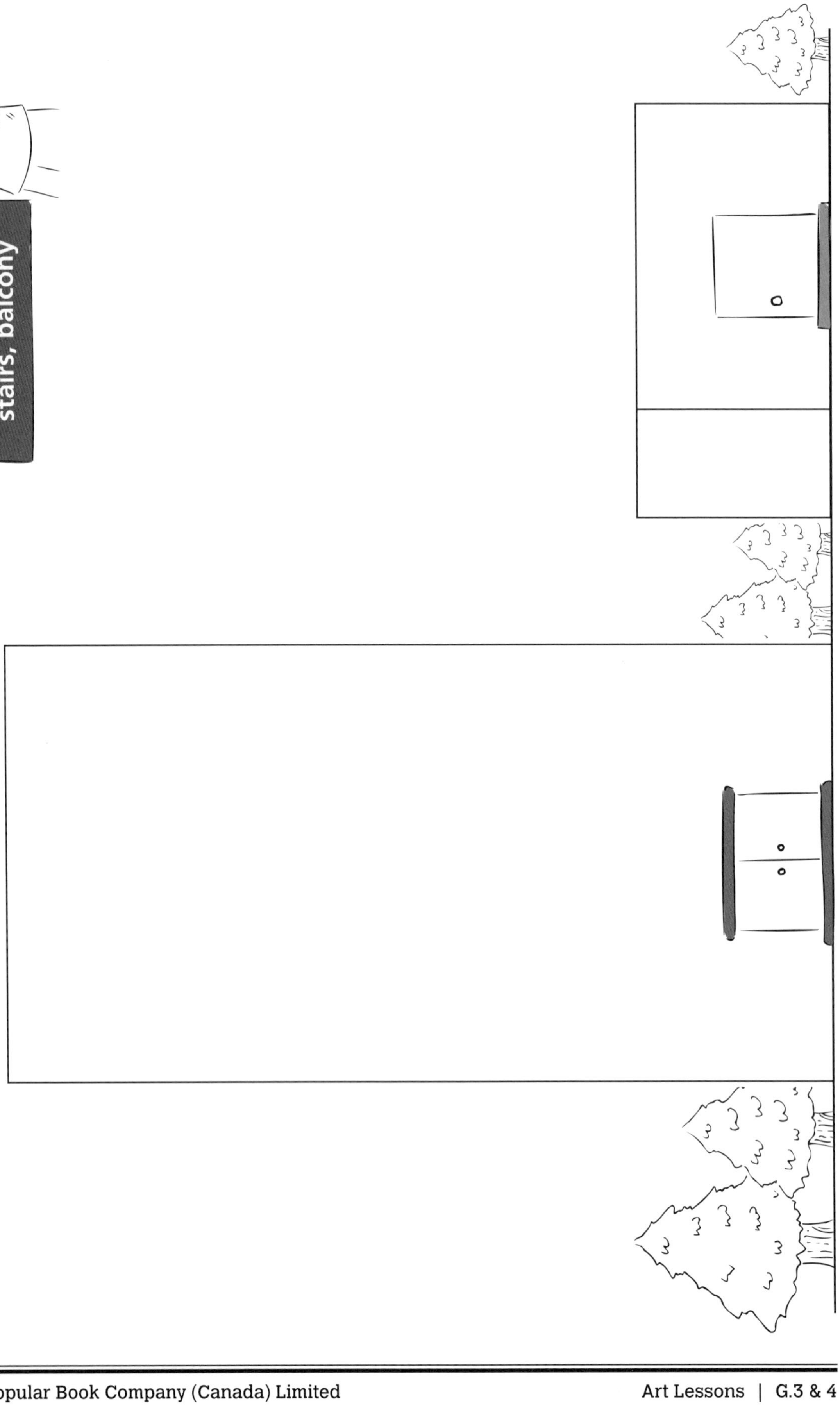

Look at the structures and decide what they are missing.
Draw the missing features on the structures.

Name: Date:

Artists' Use of Elements in Architecture

My "Tower"

Materials:

- empty tissue box
- popsicle sticks (some cut in half and quarters)
- paper rolls
- sticks/twigs/toothpicks
- cardboard
- white glue
- trays
- spray paint (optional)
- permanent markers (optional)

Motivation:

To plan a structure that has some important personal and/or historical meaning to the students (such as their house, school, church, tree house, etc.) using available materials

What to Do:

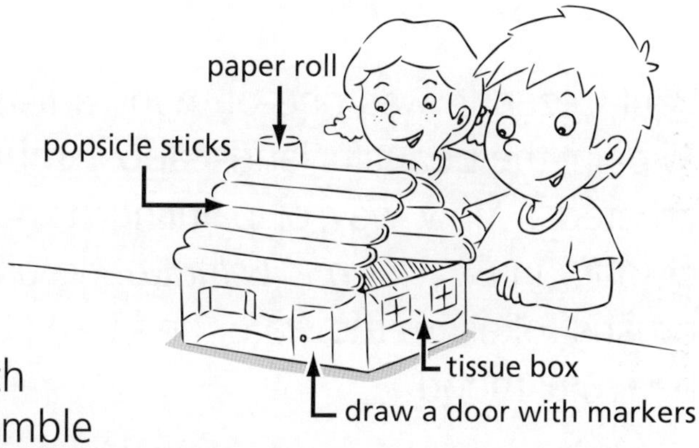

1. Have the students plan out their structure, sketching the design on paper first.

2. Use the tissue box as the base of the structure.

3. Demonstrate to students how each material can be used. (Paper rolls resemble pillars and supports. Cardboard and popsicle sticks can look like siding and roofing. Make holes for windows or apply plastic.)

4. Encourage the students to find their own uses for the materials to complete their structures. Observe and help them identify problems and possible solutions.

5. Spray paint the exterior, and detail later with permanent marker (optional).

Variations:

Have the students use their creativity to design and construct a First Nations long house, medieval castle, bridge, or other structure with these and other found materials.

Name: Date:

Observing Art

Objective: *To identify similarities and differences in content between two or more works on a related theme, to explain how the elements of design are organized in a work of art, and to communicate feelings and convey ideas*

Artists love capturing different experiences – the warmth of the sun or the cool breeze of a seaside port. Art allows us to see things through the eyes of the artist. It creates the illusion that we are part of the picture, by allowing us to sit in the seat of the master artist.

Paul Cezanne was one of many artists who loved to paint the beautiful landscapes around him. He created a new way of painting using blocks of colour. In *La Mer a L' Estaque,* he used unique brushstrokes on the water and trees to create a peaceful mood.

La Mer a L' Estaque,
Paul Cezanne, 1883-1886

Port-en-Bessin.
Georges Seurat, 1888

Georges Seurat began an original style called "pointillism". He put different coloured dots of paint next to each other to build up the homes and banks of the port he frequently visited. It is as though he wanted to make this idyllic place look out of focus or dream-like.

Name: Date:

Observing Art

Colour the sky blue and the ground green for the picture on the left, and the sky green and the ground blue for the picture on the right. Then answer the questions below.

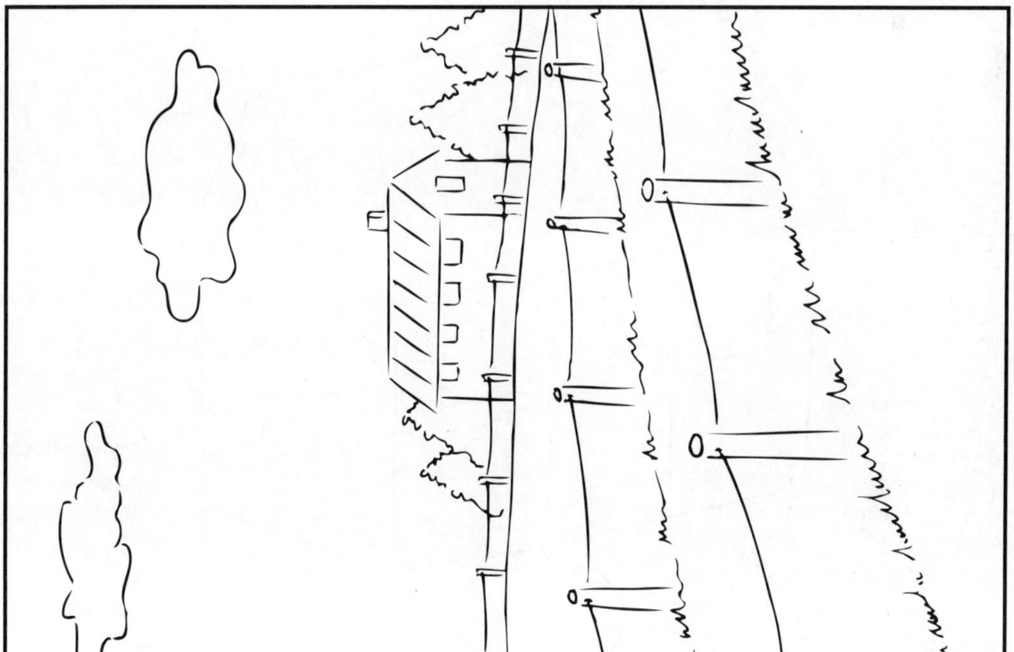

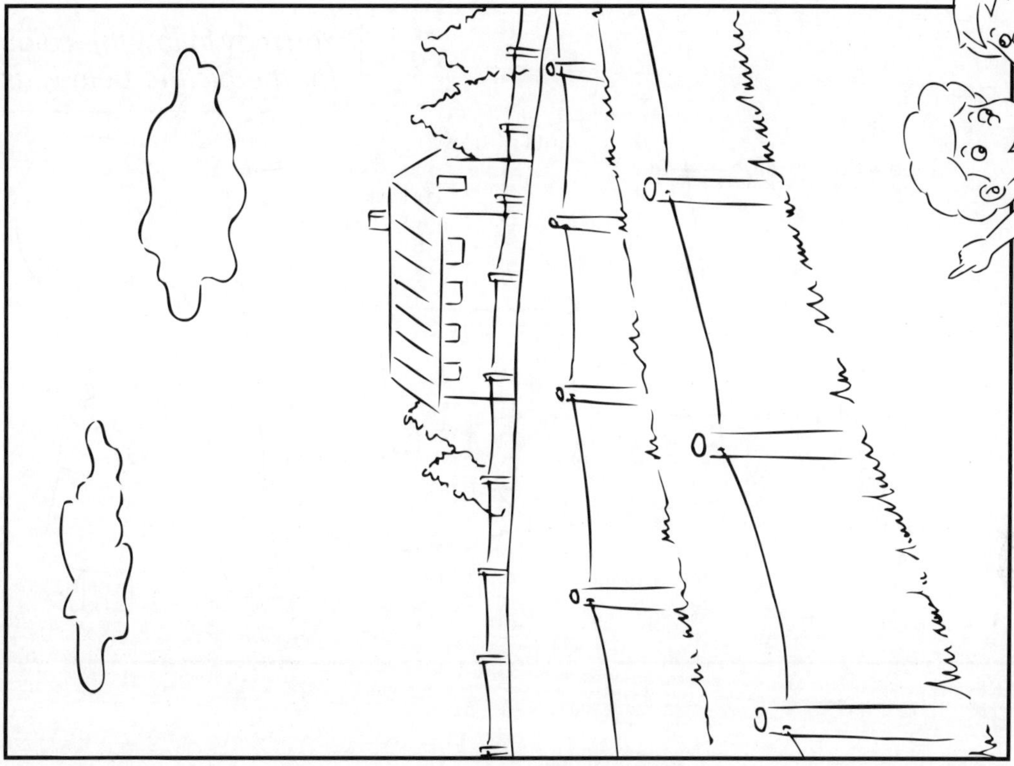

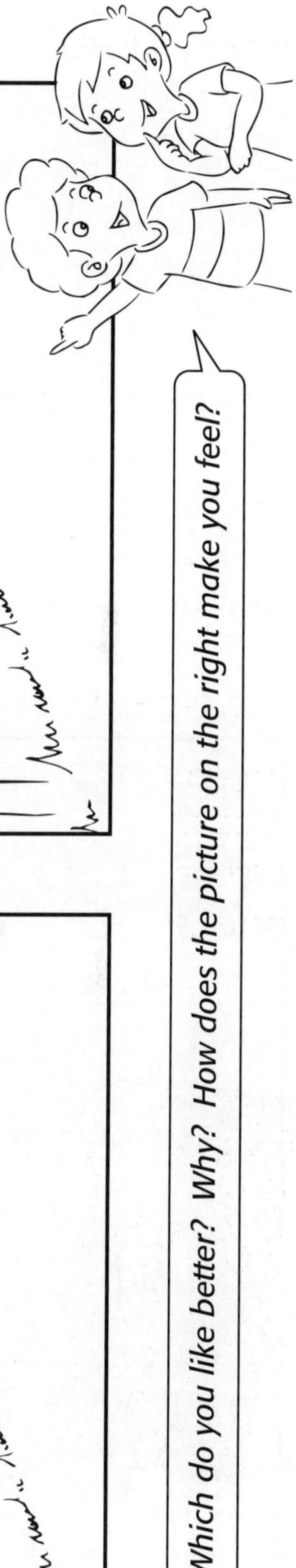

Name: Date:

Observing Art

Colour the picture using pointillism.

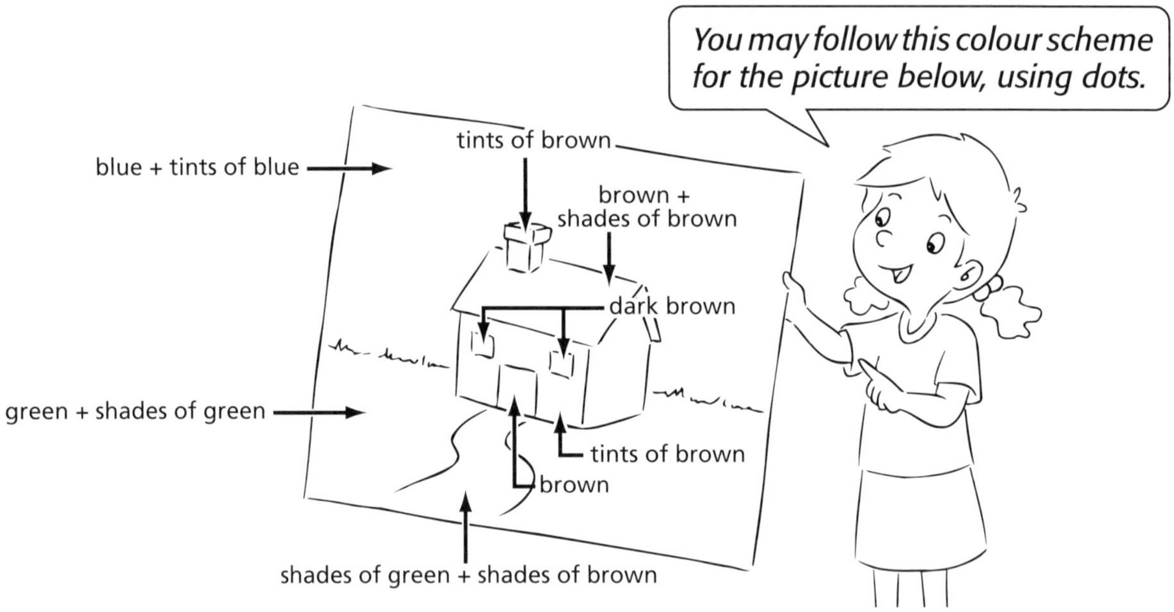

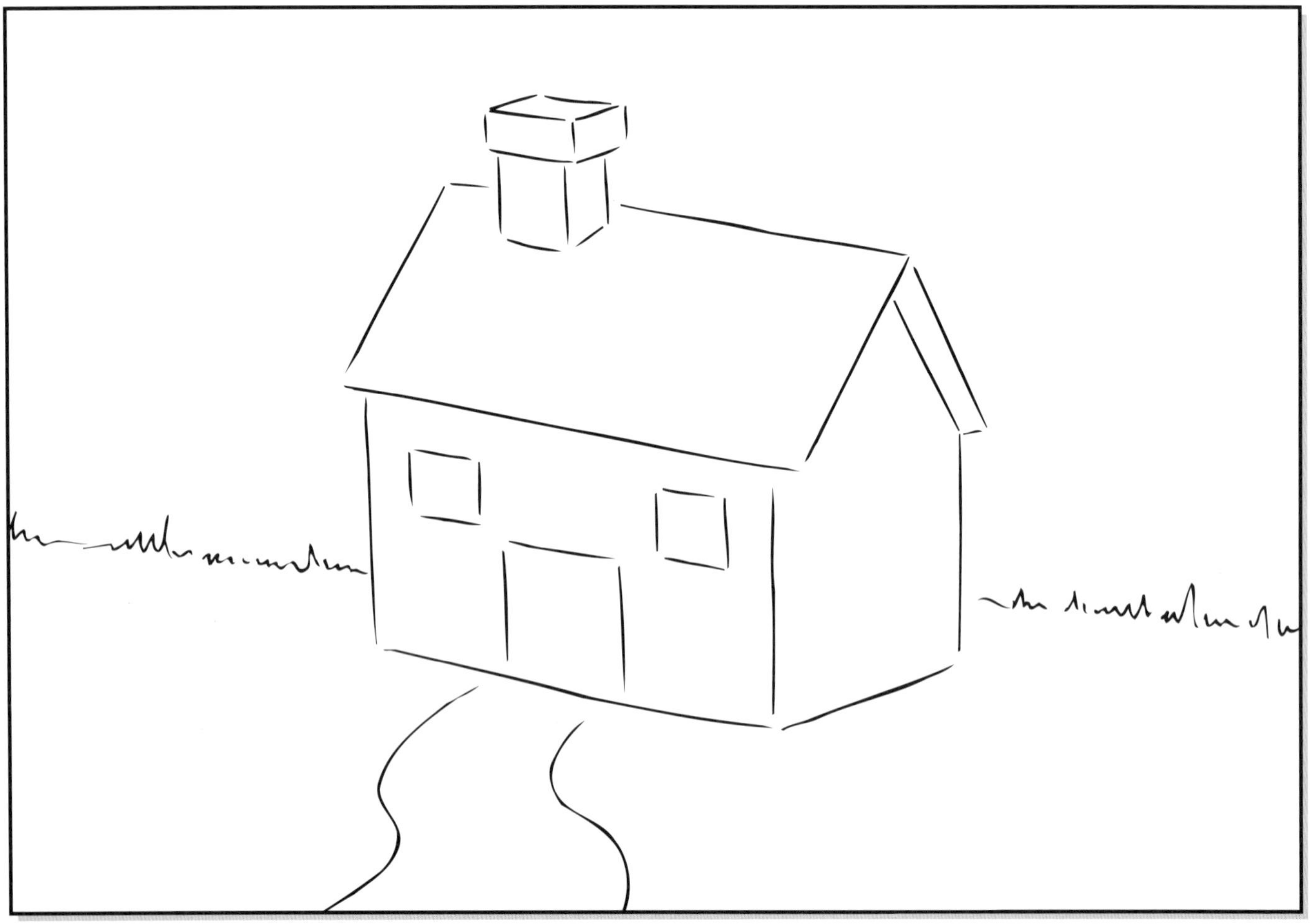

Name: Date:

Observing Art

Unique Circle Compilation

Motivation:

To create a collage of different-sized circles that illustrate differences between works that make use of the same materials

Materials:

- coloured construction paper
- circle stencils of various sizes (5-10)
- white Bristol board
- glue
- scissors

What to Do:

1. Have the students trace and cut out as many circles as they wish, using the circle stencils and scissors.
2. Cut the Bristol board in half and distribute one half to each student.
3. Get the students to glue the circles on the Bristol board in any fashion they desire (randomly, patterns, images, etc.).
4. Display all the works together when they are finished. Have the students discuss the idea that you can create very different images out of the same materials. Ask them which works they like best, and why.

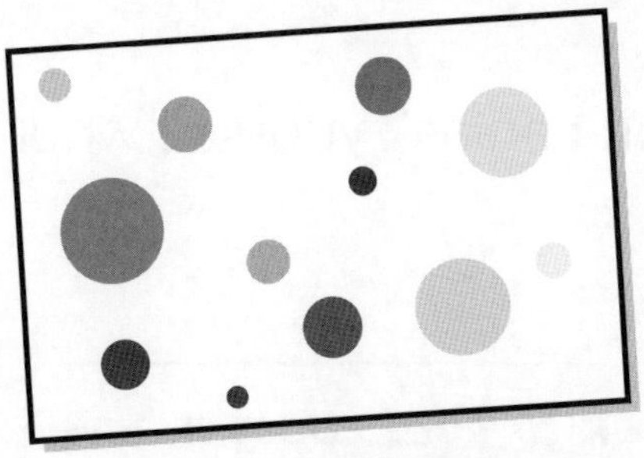
random thoughts

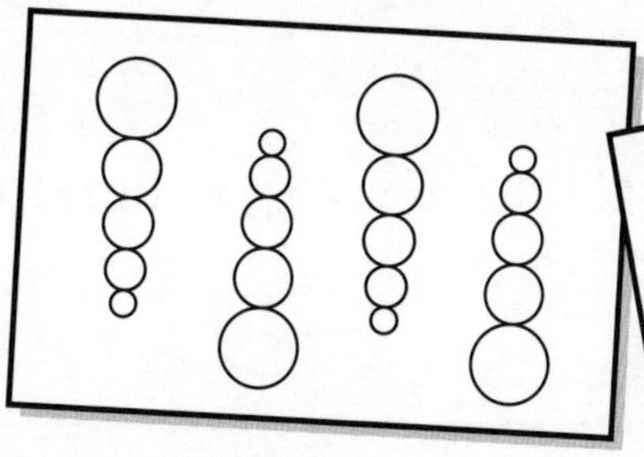
pattern with circles

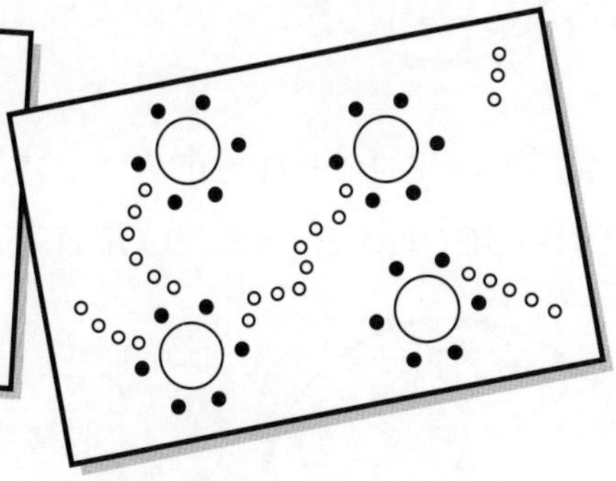
dancing flowers

Variation:

Use old magazines instead of construction paper.

Name: Date:

Evaluating Art

Objective: *To identify strengths and areas for improvement in one's own work and in others' works*

What makes some art better than other art? Why do some pieces line our museum walls and collect a fortune at auctions while others lay forgotten in someone's basement? What makes one art work stand out from the rest?

Ask yourself the following questions when considering the value of a piece of art:

How unique is it? *Is it different, special, or worth a second look?*

How does the piece reflect the artist's skill? *Does the artist use a specific technique well? How did he or she use the elements of design? Is he or she skilled?*

The final and possibly most important question that you can ask yourself when considering a piece of art is:

Does the piece touch you or speak to you? *Does it have power over the viewers, affecting their feelings or making them think? Does it leave an impression?*

If the piece of art is different, or if it shows skill or affects its audience, it will be appreciated by others.

Name: Date:

Evaluating Art

Follow the instructions below. Then answer the question.

Colour all the houses in the picture different shades of blue.

Colour the middle-most house orange and the rest in shades of blue.

What ideas are conveyed if only one object in a picture is painted with a different colour?

Name: Date:

Evaluating Art

A. Choose four elements you value most in art. Write them on the lines.

____

____

____

____

Theme Symmetry Technique
Detail Mood Illusory Texture
Effects Real Texture Colour

B. Circle either "match" or "contradict" for each case. Then identify two objects in the image that either match or contradict the indicated mood.

1.

- match / contradict
- ________________ and ________________

2.

- match / contradict
- ________________ and ________________

3.

- match / contradict
- ________________ and ________________

Name: Date:

Evaluating Art

Art Show

Imagine that your class is going to have an art show. Pick three pieces of yours that you would like to display in the show. You can also pick three pieces by somebody else in your class for this show. Don't think about WHO made the art; think about how much you like or remember it. Which six pieces will you pick?

Ask yourself these questions:

Is the art work you chose different from the rest? Is it well done? How do people respond to this piece? (Does it make others feel a certain way or think of something?)

Thinking about

My Art

1. Which three pieces would you choose?
2. Of those, which one do you like best? What do you like about this piece? What does it remind you of?
3. How was line, value, form, colour, space, or texture used to make it stand out?

Others' Art

1. Which pieces did you choose for the art show?
2. Did each piece remind you of something you like or somewhere you have been?
3. Is there something about one of these pieces that you would change?

If you were the judge of the art show, which piece would you pick as the best?

Make a journal entry explaining why you think it should win 1st place.

Art Lessons Grades 3-4

Drama and Danc

Name: Date:

The Elements of Drama

Objective: *To describe the basic elements of drama*

Think of your favourite movie. It is surely filled with actors and actresses: people whose work it is to play a role. They may show emotions that they don't really feel or talk in a way that isn't usual for them because they are taking on another personality.

People can effectively communicate a message through drama. We can learn more about other cultures or periods in history by seeing them re-enacted.

This "acting out" or drama is made up of several elements, including:

- A **character**: someone in a story.
- **Suspense**: the feeling of being unsure of what is going to happen next. It makes the drama interesting or exciting!
- The **conflict**: the problem in the story that is stressful for the characters.
- The **structure**: the plot, or how the story goes. It is like climbing a mountain. It starts at the bottom with the introduction of the people, place, and time of the story. The top of the mountain is the main problem or conflict. When this is solved, the other side of the "mountain" is reached.

We can better understand stories, poems, plays, and other materials from different cultures and times by seeing them acted out. We can even see our own sticky situations solved more clearly by "role playing" or pretending to be others.

Name: Date:

The Elements of Drama

Think of your favourite story or movie. Draw a picture of the main conflicting situation in the plot. Then write details to describe the setting of the story or movie.

My Favourite Story/Movie: ______________________

Setting

Place: ______________________

Time: ______________________

Characters: ______________________ main / supporting

______________________ main / supporting

______________________ main / supporting

Name: Date:

The Elements of Drama

Read one of the storybooks below. Then write details describing the setting, conflict, and structure of the story.

Storybooks

- **A** Goldilocks and the Three Bears
- **B** The Tortoise and the Hare
- **C** Three Little Pigs
- **D** Little Red Riding Hood

Setting

Place: ____________________

Time: ____________________

Characters: ____________________

What was the conflict?

____

____

Why did it start?

____

____

How was the conflict solved?

____

____

Name: Date:

The Elements of Drama

Making Puppets

Motivation:

To demonstrate an understanding of voice and audience by speaking as characters in a story

Materials:

- sock (in character's colour, e.g. green for snake or white for lamb)
- red or pink felt
- cardboard (from empty cereal box or thicker box)
- scissors and glue gun
- needle and thread
- variety of decorations (yarn or felt for hair, large googly eyes, etc.)

What to Do:

1. Cut out a symmetrical, oval shape approximately 1.5 cm smaller than the width of the sock from both the cardboard and the red or pink felt. Fold the cardboard in half, making it the inside of the mouth. For some animals, you could make a diamond-shaped, pointy mouth instead.
2. Insert the cardboard into the toe of the sock. Tuck the sock into the fold of the cardboard. Make a stitch in the sock and the centre of the cardboard piece to hold them together.
3. Use the pink or red felt to cover the edges of the mouth. Cut out a tongue and glue it in place.
4. Put your hand in the puppet to see the shape, and glue on ears, eyes, teeth, and other features. Use yarn or felt for hair, cutting long pieces and tying them in the centre with a shorter piece.

Follow up:

Have the students rehearse and present their short puppet theatre based on their pre-assigned or chosen story, poem, or play.

Name: Date:

Acting Out

Objective: *To demonstrate an understanding of voice and audience and the control of voice and movement by using appropriate techniques*

How can you get someone to recognize you as a pioneer from Upper Canada? How would this pioneer talk, act, or dress?

The first thing you must do to play a role is to **research the character**. Read books about your character's way of life and try to imagine what it would be like to meet someone like this.

To be believable, you must act, dress, and talk like this character. What words would this character use? Would he or she talk in a low, saddened voice, or a cheerful voice?

Use your body to "act out" what the character would do by using gestures or arm movements to make certain words stand out.

The audience has to be able to hear you from the back of the room, so speak loudly and clearly. Make your words come from your stomach area (diaphragm), and your voice will go farther. Make sure you look at the audience, moving your eyes around the room.

Step out of your shoes and into your character's so that your audience will feel as though they are actually meeting your character!

Name: Date:

Acting Out

Read the words that the characters are saying. Colour the bars to show how loud their voices should be when they read out their lines.

1. (excited) Look! The treasure is over there!

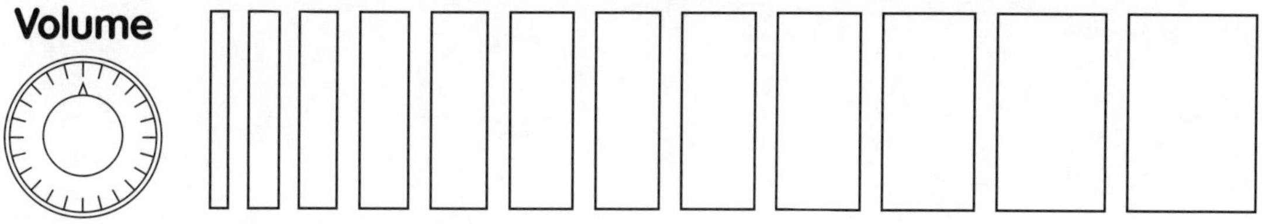

2. (low, cheerful) Laura, you are such a lovely girl!

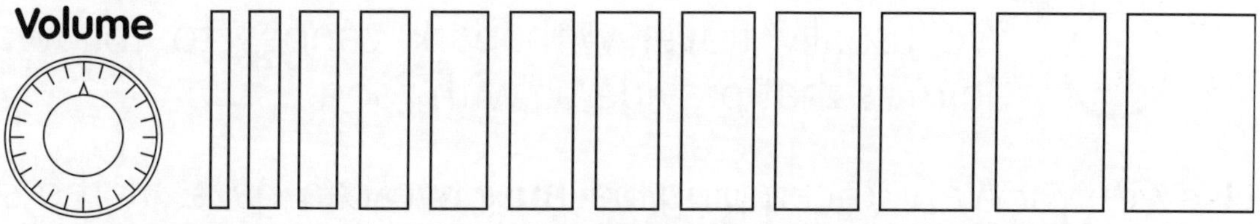

3. (whining, saddened) Who broke my porcelain doll?

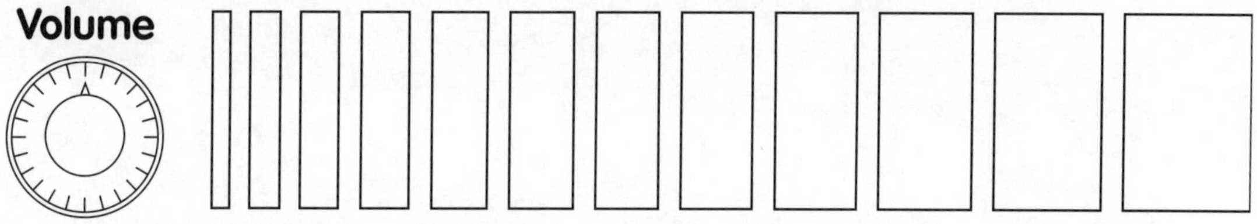

4. (delighted, delirious) I can't believe that I'm the winner!

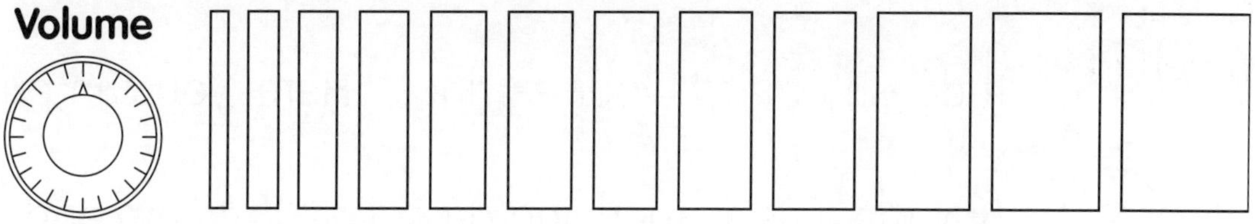

Name: Date:

Acting Out

Help each child by colouring the correct clothing he or she needs to portray the character. Then check the sentence that the character would probably say.

1.

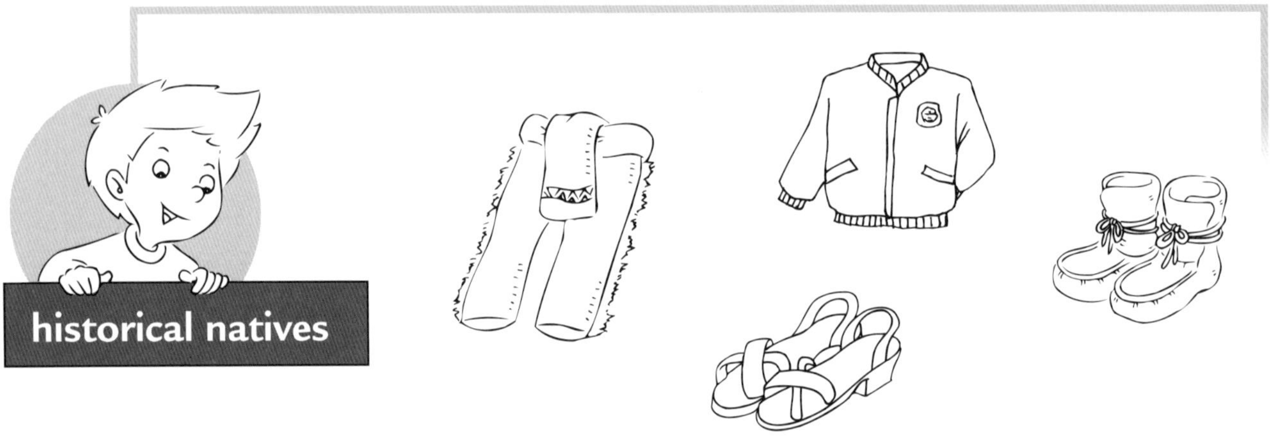

(A) We usually travel with bark canoes to follow the migrating animals that provide us with food.

(B) We like camping because we can gaze at the stars in the sky while in our sleeping bags.

2.

(A) It doesn't match your earrings. Here, you can put mine on.

(B) Buy me a new, sparkling dress or I'll scream and cry!

Name: Date:

Acting Out

Motivation:

To demonstrate an understanding of voice and audience, and to represent and interpret main characters by speaking and writing in role

Model what a historical diary page would look like. Talk about presentation skills, such as eye contact, voice projection, focus, and expression. Demonstrate how NOT to do these by starting off a lesson looking at the floor and quietly mumbling directions in a monotonous tone.

What to Do:

1 Write a lost diary page from the past. Decide what character you want to write as. Maybe it is a pioneer of Upper Canada or a medieval knight or lady.

2 Research the character, taking particular note of his or her dress, language, and activities or actions.

3 Write a diary entry detailing an event. The pioneer might be working the field. The knight might be taking part in a joust. Write it in first person (using "I", "me", and "my").

4 Practise reading your page with expression. Use a loud and clear voice. Think of what your character would do with his or her hands or body movements.

5 Present it to the class.

Name: Date:

Communicating Meaning

Objective: *To demonstrate concentration while in role and control of movement by using appropriate techniques*

There are many different ways to communicate meaning. Talking is the most obvious way to communicate, although gestures can emphasize a point and are just as effective. You will be able to get your message across far better if you practise controlling your movements. Try these great teacher-led activities to help improve your focus and movement skills.

The Sculpture and Sculptor:

The sculptor "sculpts" his or her partner into a statue of an animal by moving the partner's body into position. The sculptor pays careful attention to all of the details, and "shapes" the facial expression. When the "sculpture" is finished, the student freezes. The others guess the animal that the sculptor has created. The partners then switch roles.

Tableau:

Put students into groups of four to six to create a photo – a frozen moment in time. Each student should be aware of where the "photographer" (teacher) is and face that direction. Encourage the students to use their whole bodies to act out an animal. Have each student play a different animal to create a zoo, one group at a time. This can carry on for 15 seconds until the "photographer" says, "Snap." At this point, everyone must freeze and hold their poses, creating a **tableau**. Have the other students guess the animals. The same technique can be used to show people waiting at a bus stop, at a circus, etc.

Name: Date:

Communicating Meaning

Look at the children. Guess what animals they are pretending to be.

1.

2.

3.

4.

5.

6.

Name: Date:

Communicating Meaning

Cut out pictures of your favourite animal from old magazines or newspapers. Glue them in the box below. Write sentences to describe the movement or characteristics of the animal. Copy the action of the animal in the picture. Then perform the action in your class to see whether or not your classmates can guess what animal you are acting out.

My Favourite Animal

Name: Date:

Communicating Meaning

Animal Masks for Aesop's Fables

Materials:

- paper plates
- yarn
- markers
- glue sticks
- popsicle sticks
- felt
- feathers of different colors and sizes
- pictures of various animals' faces
- Aesop's Fables

Motivation:

To interpret and communicate the meaning of stories using drama techniques, and apply solutions to problems presented through drama and dance

What to Do:

1. Explain how masks can be used to make an act more meaningful or memorable.

2. Divide the class into group sizes appropriate for each of Aesop's Fables (e.g. one lion and one mouse). Pick fables that are less popular so that the discussion later may encourage problem solving. Have the students decide which character they would like to be; they will make a mask for this character.

3. Cut eye holes in the paper plates, and decorate the plates.

4. Glue a popsicle stick to the plate to form the handle of the face mask.

Have the students rehearse a simple, short skit retelling their fable. Use props if necessary. Discuss the idea of a "freeze frame" at the moment when the problem is clear (e.g. the lion is tied up in ropes). Encourage the audience to identify their own feelings and reactions to this situation and compare them with the characters.

Name: Date:

Marvellous Movement

Objective: *To describe basic elements of dance*

What do you feel like doing when you hear great music? Maybe your foot beats the ground a little, or you tap the table with your fingers. Does your whole body want to join in the "dance"?

Dance is a way to express ideas and feelings that are important in people's daily lives. Children have a natural desire to whirl, spin, and gallop because they love the feeling of their bodies moving.

There are several **elements** that are part of dance. These are shape, space, time (rhythm), and energy.

Shape is the body's form or group shapes. The body can produce straight or curved shapes. The arms, head, toes, and fingers can take on different shapes (e.g. open, closed, relaxed, rigid). When moving on the spot (non-locomotor) or across the floor (locomotor), your body is making shapes.

Space is the area covered by the dance movements. It is made up of **level** (distance from the ground), **direction** (up, down, forward, backward, and sideways), **pathway** (pattern that the body can make as it moves through space), and **shape**.

Time is how fast or slow the movement is, how steady or uneven it is, or how long it lasts. It includes the rhythm that your body moves to. It can be fast, medium, or slow.

Energy is the use of force while moving. It can be strong or light, sharp or smooth. Without energy, there is no dance!

Name: Date:

Marvellous Movement

Label the children's body movements and act them out.

stretching jumping bending twisting running standing still

1. ____________ 2. ____________ 3. ____________

4.

5.

6.

Name: Date:

Marvellous Movement

Follow Jenny's instructions to show movements. Then draw a picture of the shape your movements make.

1st Raise your left hand above your head.

2nd Raise your right hand, and put your palms together.

3rd Raise your right leg.

4th Put your right foot to your left knee.

5th Look at a mirror or window to check your shape.

6th Draw your shape.

Name: Date:

Marvellous Movement

Materials:

- party streamers of various colours
- chopsticks (optional)

Making Movement

Motivation:

To identify and describe examples of movement found in the students' environment and explain their uses in creative movement

A warm-up is a group of movements used to raise the core body temperature, stretch the muscles, and help focus for the dance activities to follow. Stretch or rotate the neck, shoulders, arms, upper body, waist, knees, and ankles.

What to Do:

Give each student one streamer per hand (and one chopstick per hand if you have them). Have them explore different movement possibilities, including locomotor movement (walking, running, skipping) and non-locomotor movement (bending, stretching). Encourage them to have fun with the movement of the streamers, making bigger arm movements, or using more "energy" to run faster.

Follow up:

Ask for a few volunteers to share different ways of moving, and ask them to comment on the elements they are using.

Name: Date:

Dancing around the World (I)

Objective: *To describe some aspects of dance from a variety of cultures and identify the themes and subjects found in dance works*

Is your background Russian, Mexican, Japanese, or First Nations? Maybe you have a special dance from your culture? People around the world have created wonderful, unique dances that give others a glimpse of their culture.

People have different reasons to dance, such as celebrating an event, having a good harvest, and entertaining guests. No matter what the reasons are, people like expressing their feelings and emotions through dancing. People can dance by themselves, or they can dance together to share the fun. If there are no musicians around, people can just clap their hands and stomp their feet to start a beat or rhythm. This welcomes others to follow.

Troika (Russian for "third" or "threesome") is a Russian folk dance where a man dances with two women. We can appreciate Russia by trying the *Troika*. Russia is a very cold place, and before cars were made, Russians used horses to pull sleighs. The dancers in *Troika* imitate the prancing of horses pulling a sled or carriage. *Troika* also includes a song that features strong clapping and people shouting out "Hey! Hey!" while they watch the dance. Doesn't it make you imagine fine horses galloping quickly along the cold, Russian land?

Name: Date:

Dancing around the World (I)

Find and cut out an article or a picture about a dance from a newspaper or magazine. Then write sentences to describe the features of the dance, such as movement, costumes, and the number of dancers.

Features of the Dance:

Name: Date:

Dancing around the World (I)

Follow the steps to perform the Russian dance – *Troika*. Then evaluate the performance of your group.

Troika (Steps for Every Group of Three)

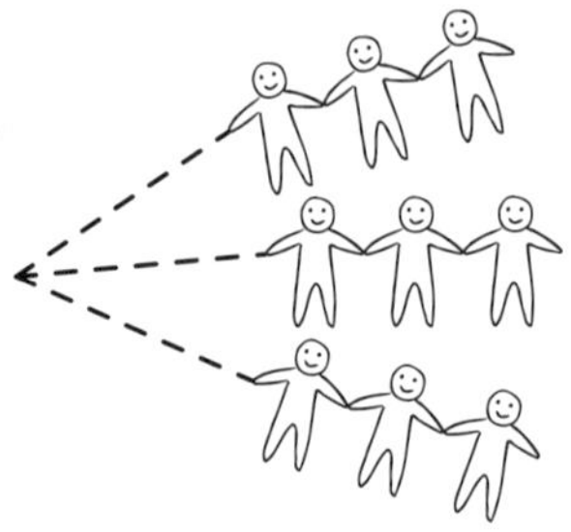

1. Each group of dancers is in a line radiating out of the centre of a circle, as if they are spokes in a wheel. Each group faces counterclockwise and joins hands.

First Section

2. While holding hands, run forward four steps on a right diagonal (right, left, right, left).
3. Run four steps forward on a left diagonal (right, left, right, left).
4. Run forward for eight counts.

Second Section

5. Groups continue to hold hands. B and C raise their common hands and form a bridge. A goes under the bridge and B follows, rotating hands loosely to end up in starting position.
6. Repeat step 5 making the bridge with A and B while C goes under.

Third Section

7. Groups of three join hands to form a small circle. Run 12 steps to the left, stamp 3 times in place.
8. Run 12 steps to the right, and open the lines to the beginning formation on the last 3 stamps.

Self-evaluation

- Body awareness (what the body does, its actions) ____________
- Space awareness (where the body moves, such as its directions) ____________
- Body movements (relationship of the body to other individuals) ____________
- Qualities (how the body moves in terms of time, flow) ____________

Name: Date:

Dancing around the World (I)

Materials:

- *Troika* recording

Motivation:

To know more about the steps, music, and costumes of this Russian dance – Troika

What to Do:

1 Play the *Troika*. Discuss what this music "looks" like. Then have the students explore the answers to the following questions.

2 a. What will the speed of the steps be?

b. How will the space be used?

c. What instruments do you think might make the music?

d. How do you imagine the dancers dress?

After the discussion, let the students try to dance *Troika* with the music on, and remind them to imagine themselves in the wintertime of Russia, in a sleigh pulled by horses.

Name: Date:

Dancing around the World (II)

Objective: *To describe some aspects of dance from a variety of cultures and identify the themes and subjects found in dance works*

The *Jarabe Tapatio*

Many people in Mexico dress in brilliantly coloured, light clothing, which reflects Mexico's mostly hot and sunny weather. It also becomes a kind of costume for the *Jarabe Tapatio*, or Mexican Hat Dance, a dance that symbolizes the national pride and honour of the Mexican people. Mexicans use the Mexican guitar, trumpets, and violins to make their music lively.

The *Hora*

The *Hora* is the national dance of Israel. When the music, called *Hava Nagila,* is played, everyone joins in and forms a circle holding hands. To start the dance, people step forward toward the right with the left foot, and then follow with the right foot. The left foot is then brought back, followed by the right foot. Everyone moves in a fast, cheerful, and circular motion to the right.

It is customary to raise the person (or people) of honour on a chair while the music is playing. This is done at many Jewish and Israeli weddings. Dancing the *Hora* together can make us feel as though we have something to celebrate!

Name: Date:

Dancing around the World (II)

This is a two-page activity. Do a little research to find out what Mexicans like to wear or what instruments they like to play when performing the *Jarabe Tapatio*. Colour the correct clothing and instruments on page 140 . Then cut them out and glue them on the characters below.

Ready for the *Jarabe Tapatio*:

Name: Date:

Dancing around the World (II)

Ready for the *Jarabe Tapatio*:

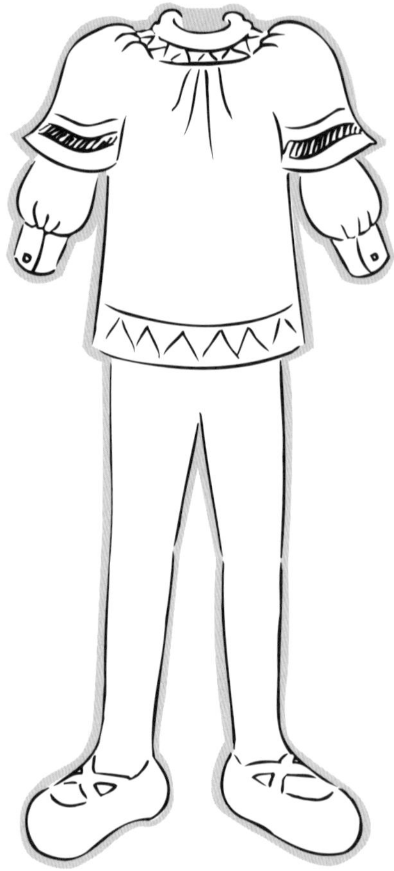

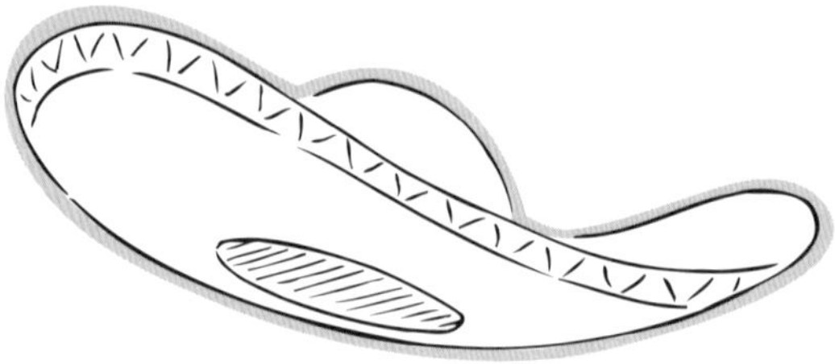

Name: Date:

Dancing around the World (II)

Materials:

- *Hora* recording

Motivation:

To know more about the steps, music, and costumes of the Israeli dance, the Hora

What to Do:

Play the *Hora*. Discuss what this music "looks" like. Then have the students explore the answers to the following questions:

1. What will the speed of the steps be?
2. How will the space be used?
3. What instruments do you think might make the music?
4. How do you imagine the dancers dress?

Steps to Dance:

1. Everyone holds hands to form a circle.
2. Step forward toward the right with the left foot.
3. Follow with the right foot.
4. Bring back the left foot, followed by the right foot.

Art Lessons Grades **3-4**

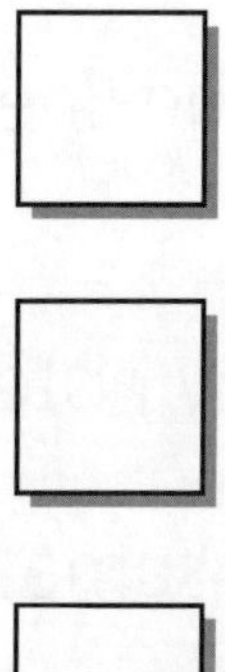

Checklists

Name: Date:

Checklist: Music

- ☐ I can demonstrate the difference between the terms "beat" and "rhythm".
- ☐ I can indicate with appropriate arm movements the dynamics heard in familiar music.
- ☐ I can recognize that sounds and silences of different durations may be represented by symbols.
- ☐ I can identify whole notes, half notes, quarter notes, and eighth-notes.
- ☐ I can recognize that the treble clef defines the names of the lines and spaces on the staff.
- ☐ I can recognize that specific pitches may be represented by notes.
- ☐ I know that unison is two notes on the same line or in the same space and sung or played simultaneously.
- ☐ I can communicate thoughts and feelings about the music I hear using proper terminology and can explain my preferences for specific songs.
- ☐ I can identify the tone colour in familiar music.
- ☐ I can identify the individual instruments of the woodwind, brass, string, and percussion families.
- ☐ I can create an accompaniment for a story, poem, or drama presentation, using my knowledge of beat, rhythm, and tone colour.

Name: Date:

Checklist: Visual Arts

- ☐ I can recognize and name the warm and cool colours and describe their emotional impact.
- ☐ I can identify the characteristics of a variety of lines.
- ☐ I can label a piece's foreground, middle ground, and background, and can identify objects in each of these areas of a work of art.
- ☐ I can identify symmetrical and asymmetrical shapes in the human-made environment and in the natural world.
- ☐ I know the difference between real and illusory textures.
- ☐ I know the elements of design and can identify them in a variety of natural and human-made environments.
- ☐ I can use art tools, materials, and techniques correctly to create different effects.
- ☐ I can identify monochromatic colour schemes.
- ☐ I know the emotional qualities of lines.
- ☐ I know that overlapping shapes is a way of creating the illusion of depth.
- ☐ I can distinguish between relief and free-standing sculptures.
- ☐ I can describe the way artists use a variety of tools, materials, and techniques to create texture.
- ☐ I know the strengths and limitations of a variety of familiar art tools, materials, and techniques.
- ☐ I know how to use art tools, materials, and techniques properly, with control, singly and in combination with each other.

Name: Date:

Checklist: Drama and Dance

- ☐ I understand a character's point of view through writing, speaking, and using body movements in role.
- ☐ I can describe my own and others' work in drama and dance using appropriate vocabulary.
- ☐ I can demonstrate the ability to concentrate while in role in drama and dance.
- ☐ I can recognize and choose appropriate elements of movement for dramatizing my responses to different stimuli or ideas.
- ☐ I can describe the kinds of energy involved in a sequence of movement.
- ☐ I can distinguish between varieties of dance forms using specific criteria.
- ☐ I have knowledge of voice and audience when speaking and writing in role as a character in a story.
- ☐ I can identify and describe examples of movement found in my environment and explain their use in creative movement.
- ☐ I can describe aspects of dances from a variety of cultures.
- ☐ I am aware of the need to do warm-up exercises before engaging in dance activities.

Art Lessons Grades 3-4

Project Ideas

Name: Date:

Mirror Image

Through this exercise, students will learn to imitate and follow another person. Additionally, students learn to anticipate what the other person might do and take on another state of mind.

What to Do:

1. Pair up your students.
2. Have them stand face to face about one foot apart.
3. Choose one person from each pair to "lead", making movements for his/her partner to copy.
4. Make sure the movements are interesting and slow enough for partners to mime, as if they were a reflection in a full-length mirror.
5. Swap partners after enough time has passed.

Name: Date:

Bear Cave

Materials:

- dry leaves or plastic leaves
- a big carton
- stuffed bears of different sizes

What to Do:

1 Set the box up in the dramatic play area (or in a corner of the room).

2 Put the leaves inside the cave and outside as well.

3 Put the stuffed bears in the cave.

4 Review hibernation with your students, and then allow them to act it out with the materials.

Addition:

Give the children earth-coloured crayons to make cave drawings inside the "bear cave".

Name: Date:

Make Your Own Egg Shakers

Materials:

- two hollow, plastic eggs that come apart
- rice, pebbles, lentils, seeds, kidney beans
- masking tape
- glue
- tissue paper

What to Do:

1 For each hollow egg, fill the bottom of each with rice, lentils, seeds, or kidney beans.

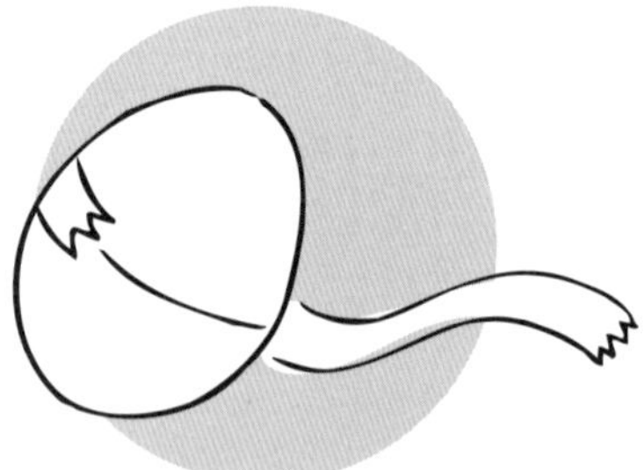

2 Fasten the top to the bottom and tape the seal so that the top and bottom will not separate when the egg is shaken.

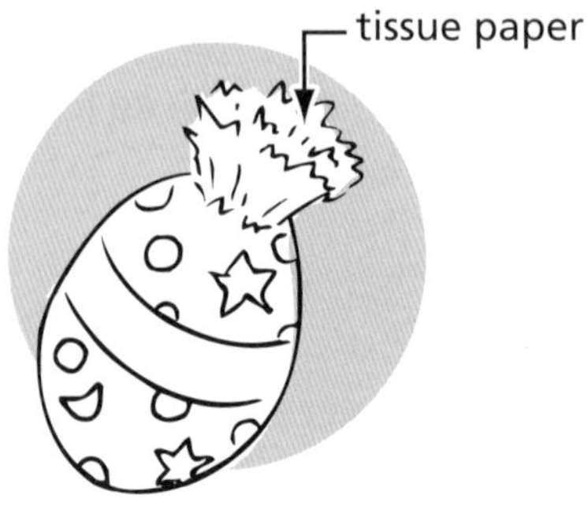

3 Apply the glue to the surface of the egg. Wrap the egg with tissue paper for decoration. You may also add some stickers to decorate your egg.

4 When dry, shake each egg and note that they all have different sounds.

Name: Date:

Make Your Own Pan Flute

Materials:

- six drinking straws
- tape (masking or electrical)
- modelling clay
- ribbon
- ruler
- glue and scissors

What to Do:

1. Measure and cut the straws into the following lengths:

17.5 cm,	15.5 cm,	13.5 cm,	12.5 cm,	11 cm,	10 cm,	9 cm,	8.5 cm
Do	Re	Mi	Fa	So	La	Ti	Do

2. Cover one end of each straw with a piece of modelling clay. Make sure no air can get through the covered end.
3. Align the straws from longest to shortest with all of the open ends facing the same way, forming a straight line across. Then apply the masking tape to the straws about 2 cm down from the straight alignment.
4. Tape the other side in the same way so that the straws are securely fastened together and stay in a straight line.
5. Put the glue on the masking tape and apply the ribbon. The ribbon should cover the masking tape.
6. Let dry.
7. Blow across the top of the open ended straws and listen to the changes in pitch as you blow into each straw.

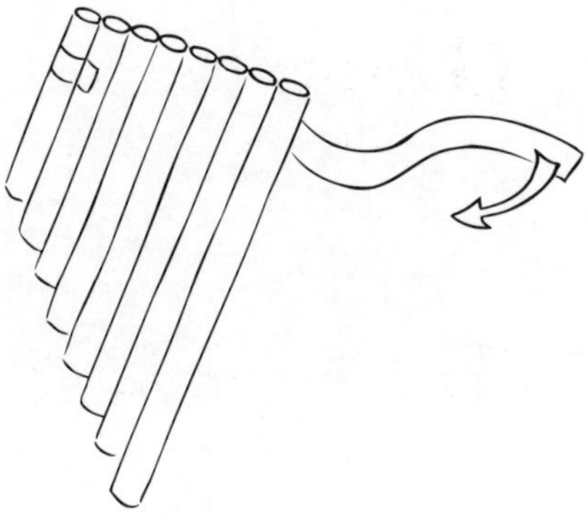

Name: Date:

Space

You will have a better understanding of the terms foreground, middle ground, and background after completing this drawing.

Materials:

- tracing paper
- pencil
- tape
- crayons; coloured pencils

What to Do:

1. Tape the tracing paper to a window where there are not large obstructions and where you can make out a foreground, middle ground, and background.

2. Trace what you see within the limits of the paper.

3. Remove your drawing from the window and colour it delicately.

Name: Date:

Similarities and Differences

What to Do:

1 Identify the similarities and differences between the pictures below.

2 Colour the similarities using the same colour in both images and the differences using a different colour.

3 Describe how the differences change the images. (e.g. the way the water is moving, or how the sun is shining)

Materials:

- crayons
- coloured pencils
- paper
- a pen

Name: Date:

Practise Your Drawing!

Follow the steps to draw the pictures. You may add your own details to the pictures to make them more unique!

Animals

1. **Pig**

2. **Elephant**

3. **Panda**

Name: Date:

Practise Your Drawing!

Plants

1. **Sunflower**

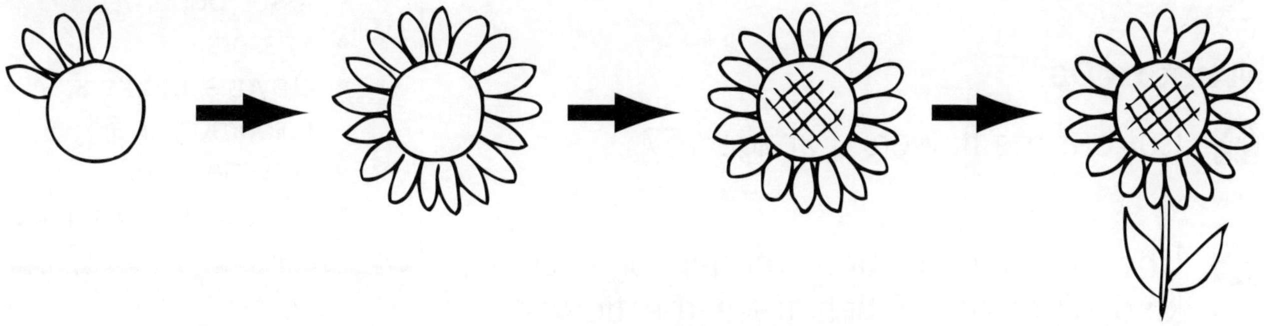

2. **Cactus**

3. **Palm Tree**

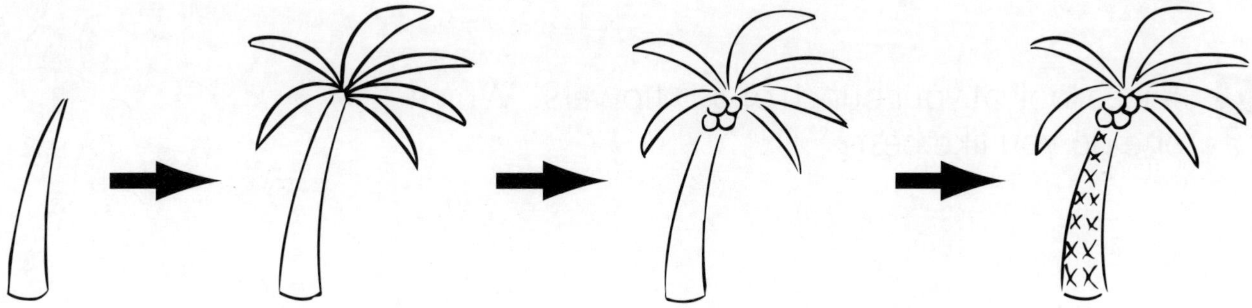

Name: Date:

3-D Overlapping Flowers

Use different materials to make overlapping 3-D flowers.

Materials:

- Bristol board
- construction paper
- tissue paper
- scissors
- crayons, markers, coloured pencils
- pipe cleaners
- buttons with big holes

What to Do:

1 Cut out the flowers on page 157.

2 Choose your favourite model for each kind of flower. Then trace the flower petals onto your chosen material and cut them out.

3 Assemble the petals so that each (X) is aligned.

4 Puncture the X through the middle of the "flower" for the stem.

5 Insert the pipe cleaner through the holes of the button.

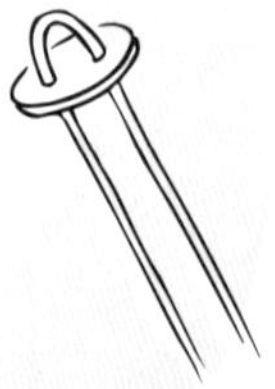

6 Insert the pipe cleaners in the button through the hole in the flower petals. Secure the petals to the pipe cleaner by twisting the pipe cleaners together at the base of the petals.

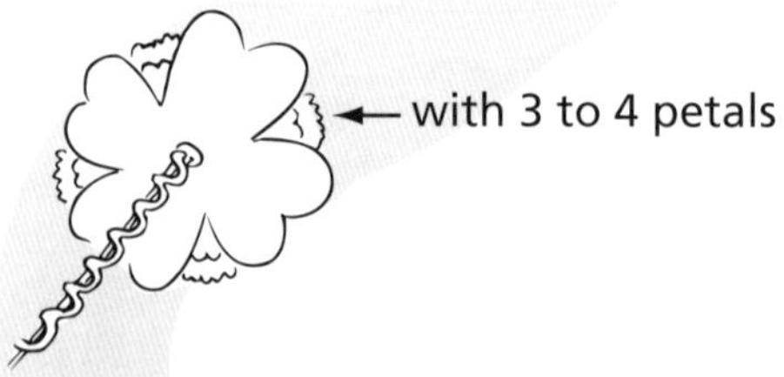

7 Take a look at your bunch of 3-D flowers! Which one do you like best?

Name: Date:

3-D Overlapping Flowers

Flower Stencils:

Name: Date:

Glittering Fish

Materials:

- Bristol board
- glue stick
- aluminum foil
- scissors
- acrylic paint
- paintbrushes and plate
- cardboard

What to Do:

1 Cut out each part of the fish and the scale stencil on page 159.

2 Trace each part of the fish on the Bristol board. Then cut them out.

3 Trace many scales onto the Bristol board and aluminum foil. Then cut them out.

4 Glue the foil scales onto the Bristol board scales. Repeat until you have enough scales to cover the body of the fish.

5 Glue the body of the fish onto the cardboard.

6 Glue the fish scales, foil side up, to the fish body. Start at the tail, overlapping them as you go.

7 Glue the face, fins, and tail to the body.

8 Paint the face, fins, and tail with the acrylic paint.

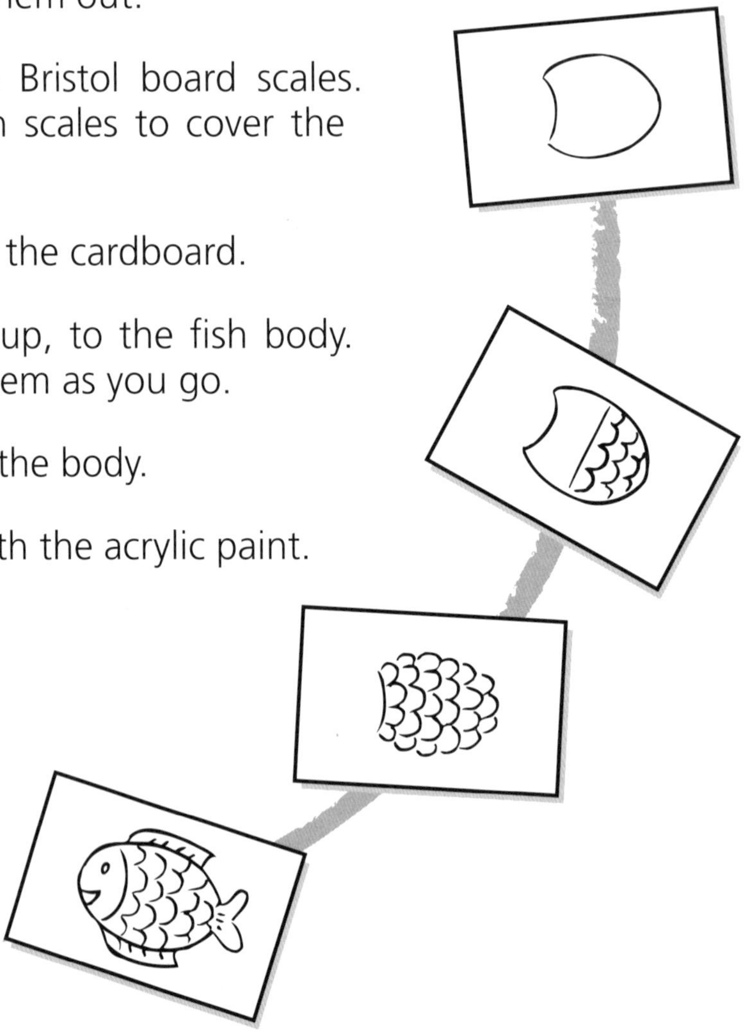

Name: Date:

Glittering Fish

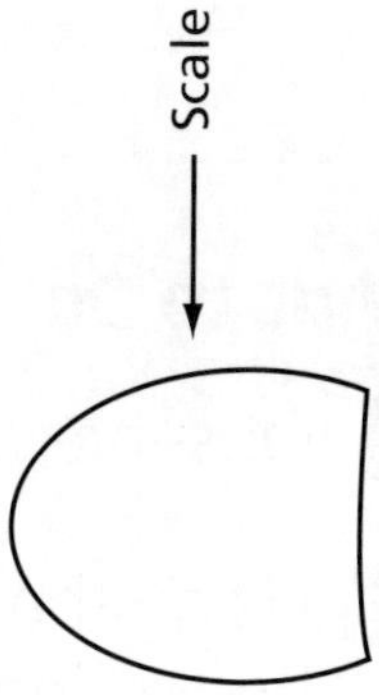

Name: Date:

What Is Different?

Colour the pictures and answer the question.

Materials:

- crayons
- coloured pencils
- pen
- paper

What to Do:

1 Observe the vase with flowers.

2 Using the basic structure of the flowers in the first picture, recreate the flowers by adding your own details and differentiating them from the first picture to change the feeling of the overall bouquet.

3 Write down what you did differently and the effects it created. (e.g. Does the bouquet look fuller? Do the flowers look softer?, etc.)